Journal of Practical Ethics

 VOLUME 9, NUMBER 2. MARCH 2022

The Journal of Practical Ethics is available online, free of charge, at:
http://jpe.ox.ac.uk and https://journals.publishing.umich.edu/jpe/

Editorial Policy
The *Journal of Practical Ethics* is an invitation only journal. Papers are anonymously appraised prior to publication by expert reviewers who are not part of the editorial staff. It is entirely open access online, and print copies may be ordered at cost price via a print-on-demand service. Authors and reviewers are offered an honorarium for accepted articles. The journal aims to bring the best in academic moral and political philosophy, applied to practical matters, to a broader student or interested public audience. It seeks to promote informed, rational debate, and is not tied to any one particular viewpoint. The journal will present a range of views and conclusions within the analytic philosophy tradition. It is funded through the generous support of the *Uehiro Foundation in Ethics and Education.*

CONTENTS

———————●•●———————

ᴓ JPE ᴓ

Précis of *Evil Online*

DEAN COCKING
Delft Design for Values Institute

JEROEN VAN DEN HOVEN
Delft University of Technology

Evil Online begins with the story of the ship *Batavia* that was wrecked off the coast of Western Australia early in the seventeenth century.[1] About 150 people survived the wreck to reach a deserted island. However, over the next few months, Jeronimus Cornelisz, imbued with ideas about being beyond good and evil and harboring mutinous motives from the start, led others on a reign of terror. They murdered most of the survivors, including many women and children. According to some of the few who lived to tell the tale, the murders often seemed to be done just for the fun of it.

Many evils online have emerged in similar ways. Attitudes and conduct are set in new, unfamiliar worlds where the voices of moral authorities and the constraints of existing social institutions are often too weak to be heard, and isolation from the reactions of others is ubiquitous. Unsurprisingly, those already guided by antisocial and immoral attitudes have been able to run amok online. However, many who were not already so inclined have also gone astray. Worries about the flourishing of evil online are not confined to violations of values or to the enabling of our darker sides—they are also about the undermining of our 'better angels' and about losing sight of our values altogether. Establishing that there are these more fundamental dangers and trying to better understand this territory of evildoing—not fully explained by the rule of preexisting antisocial attitudes—are the main aims of the book.

---

1. Dean Cocking and Jeroen van den Hoven, *Evil Online* (New York: Wiley, 2018).

Contact: Dean Cocking <dean.cocking@bigpond.com>
    ⓘ https://orcid.org/0000-0002-2590-4925
    Jeroen van den Hoven <M.J.vandenHoven@tudelft.nl>
    ⓘ https://orcid.org/0000-0003-2376-3185

https://doi.org/10.3998/jpe.2376

The most influential contemporary description of the evildoing of people not already of antisocial minds has been Hannah Arendt's account of the 'banality of evil'. On this account, or a common reading of it, people can become evildoers because they are fundamentally unthinking and uncritical about their conduct. Their attitudes and pursuits may have ordinary, widely shared, seemingly morally neutral descriptions, such as 'doing one's job well' since they possess, Arendt says, 'an inability to think, namely to think from the standpoint of someone else'.[2]

Much of the rise of evil online may be seen as providing spectacular, new, and widespread ways in which evil is banal and can flourish. Certainly, evil seems commonly committed without the perpetrators(s) recognizing the evilness of their conduct (much less their being motivated by, or aiming at, the evil they commit). But such failures of people to recognize the evil in what they do is typically not *simply* banal. Invariably, much more needs to be said in order to explain the apparent banality of evil and how 'unthinkingness' can enable evil (and sometimes the evil is not really banal at all). In order to provide this further and additional explanation, *Evil Online* argues that such failures of moral understanding about the realities of one's conduct, and how these failures enable evildoing, is better understood in terms of agency being undertaken in a 'moral fog'.

The moral fog of our online social worlds results from the coalescence of a cluster of features that shape self-expression and communication, such as the algorithms; the business models of online platforms; their design for personalization[3] and addiction, to be engaged in relentless self/other comparisons, to have 'weak ties' with one another, and to be isolated from the reactions of others and from broader and conflicting views; the collapsing of the public and private realms on social media platforms; the virtual reality of the medium; and the seeming anonymity.

In addition, the new digital technology comes with significant 'interpretative flexibility'. Revolutionary technology typically creates very new environments where attitudes and norms are yet to be settled. As a result, moral uncertainty and confusion can reign until some closure has been reached about the nature and purpose of the technology. The Internet is a striking example of technology bringing interpretative flexibility, and plainly much uncertainty and confusion remains. These various features (and others) of online environments and how they shape self-expression and communication are described

---

2. Hannah Arendt, *Eichmann in Jerusalem* (London: Penguin, 1964), p. 49.

3. Personalization (e.g., through the targeting of information and advertisements on the basis of our revealed interests and preferences).

in chapter 2. In particular, many of the features of online environments that are identified are used to help explain the creation of moral fog online and how it enables evil.

Chapter 1 introduces (some of) the many faces of evil online, such as radicalization, cyber bullying, glorification of anorexia, digital self-harm, misogyny, racism, revenge porn, shaming, catfishing, and sick prankster vloggers. Across many of these cases, beyond long-standing crimes such as theft, blackmail, and fraud, preexisting antisocial attitudes (e.g., of self-gain or due to mental illness) do not provide much of an explanation. Instead, very banal drivers and attitudes are commonplace, such as getting lost in and being unthinking about one's particular online environment, going to more extreme behaviors so as to be included or stand out in one's scene, or because 'It was fun' or 'I could' or 'everyone else was doing it'.

Chapter 3 provides an account of negative impacts the online social revolution has effected broadly across some of our basic values—in particular, autonomy, intimacy, privacy, civility, and trust. The losses and distortions of these values are described and accounted for as resulting from a notable 'demolition job' the online social revolution has effected upon our traditional abilities to cohabit the generally quite separate, very different, and often contrasting worlds of public and private life. The discussion illustrates how the territory of our traditional lives across these fronts has enabled key aspects of our basic values and how, with the loss and distortion of our plural worlds of public and private life online, so too there has been a loss and distortion of these values.

Chapter 3 also describes how a common driver for users online is the idea that one can seemingly pursue life far more on 'one's own terms' (i.e., relatively unhindered by the influence of others and the conventions, laws, and settings of one's traditional world). Various design features of online social worlds, such as personalization and isolation, especially enable users to think they are 'masters of their domain' in such ways. While this outlook has long been a very seductive driver in our *off*line worlds, and it is well exploited across online social platforms, the discussion describes how it is also fundamentally antisocial and corrupts individual moral character.

Evil Online develops the idea of moral fog to provide an explanatory umbrella across a broad range of evils, both online and in our traditional worlds. Chapters 4 and 5 develop the account of the moral fog of evil and also the accounts of moral character and the prosocial life to which the discussion has led. Chapter 4 describes varieties of moral fog in our traditional lives. The account of moral fog is developed here in relation to Arendt's banality thesis and the social science experiments of Stanley Milgram, Philip Zimbardo, and others and the various associated lessons and analyses taken from these experiments.

The discussion in chapter 4 also highlights how the shared life, usually discussed in terms of providing the well-springs of the good life, just as well can create moral fog that enables a variety of long-standing evils. So, for instance, while our needs for intimacy and our learning and developmental dependence upon others provides the impetus for some key goods of the shared life, they also provide notable sources of moral obfuscation and corruption.

Evil Online draws attention to various ways in which individual moral character is crucially socially constructed and dependent, in particular, upon the territory of self-expression and communication we have been navigating for millennia. Chapter 5 develops this approach to moral character and the prosocial life in counterpoint to some common views about moral character, its relations to self-interest, and the oft-imagined independence of moral character from reliance upon others and conditions of the external world.

The book concludes with a focus on the fate of moral character in an age where so much of the complexity and nuance of the social territory upon which the moral life has long been developed has been distorted and replaced by social media platforms—platforms that support the illusion of pursuing life on one's own terms and enable the construction of individual character and the shared life to be increasingly defined by 'just me and the Internet'.

◣JPE◢

Moral Intensifiers and the Efficiency of Communication

DALE DORSEY
University of Kansas

Keywords: communication, intensity, moral theory, internet.

I was very pleased to be asked to read and to comment on *Evil Online*, which strikes me as a timely and important moral investigation of our era. Computers interconnected with each other, whether it be by dial-in message board or the Reddit app on our smartphones, fundamentally alter the way people communicate. We communicate, simply put, more efficiently. And with this change in methods of communication comes changes in the way our moral world is organized.

For Cocking and van den Hoven, this change is for the worse. Online worlds create, in their view, a kind of 'moral fog', one that leads to a special kind of 'evildoing'. Our lives online—for various reasons, they discuss—draw us (or, at least, some of us) away from a 'prosocial' mindset to one that is much more susceptible to harm, whether directed to self or other. They write, 'Our online-transformed worlds have delivered new and widespread forms of moral fog that limit and negatively shape moral imagination and understanding' (147).

However, or so I shall argue in this brief commentary, I think that while Cocking and van den Hoven are correct to investigate the moral effects of our online existence, and are quite obviously correct to be concerned about the potential for evil such online worlds present, the online worlds we inhabit are diverse and morally complicated. In particular, I will argue that the same features of our online existence that engender evildoing also give rise to important instances of moral progress and moral good. In short, there is nothing

Contact: Dale Dorsey <ddorsey@ku.edu>
ⓘ https://orcid.org/0000-0002-7184-6703

https://doi.org/10.3998/jpe.2377

inherently *evil* about the change in our world given its *e*-ness. However, or so it seems to me, one thing about which Cocking and van den Hoven are certainly correct is that online communities present a kind of unpredictable *intensification* of our moral atmosphere, likely displaying features characteristic of many technological advances in communication, and that presents unique features of its own.

The Efficiency of Communication

What, at heart, makes our online worlds different than the worlds we occupy in the 'real world'? What makes *cyber*space a distinct moral environment?

Cocking and van den Hoven suggest that there are a number of features that render our lives online particularly susceptible to evildoing (43–58). However, one might understand each of these characteristics under a more general heading. What distinguishes our online lives, at least in those corridors of the Internet that Cocking and van den Hoven identify as being especially susceptible to evildoing, is the *efficiency of communication*. Communication—sending information from one person to another, whether this is by text, video, audio, or any other medium—is simply more efficient than it has ever been. It is virtually costless to the end user (beyond the general costs they pay for data access). It is *instantaneous*. It is or can be *anonymous* (further reducing its costs). Couple these with the fact that it is possible to reach an extremely large audience, depending on one's forum, and that this audience is worldwide. Furthermore, it is possible to communicate directly with those whose interests, proclivities, and so on are your targets but also to do so without doing substantial research on how to communicate with those people in particular. (To communicate with fans of the heavy metal band Iron Maiden, for example, one needn't set up a lengthy and costly mail sign-up sheet or run advertisements on heavy metal radio—in itself inefficient insofar as it would speak to fans of Metallica also. One need only look to the subreddit r/IronMaiden or post to the wall of the official Iron Maiden Facebook group.) In addition, the end user can have sophisticated algorithms tailor just what sort of information and communication they wish to consume or would be interested in consuming, further reducing the cost of communication between people. If, for instance, I am a manufacturer of boutique oven mitts and I want to get the word out, I can have a social media algorithm present information about my company just to those people who are likely to be most interested.

But put in this way, one might initially be skeptical that the Internet as a tool is, per se, conducive to evildoing or good-doing. It is, after all, a tool for efficient communication. So why should we think that this generally pushes us toward goodness or evil? Cocking and van den Hoven suggest that there are key features of the Internet that are redefining our social world (60) and introducing a moral fog that tends to lead people away from the prosocial and toward evil-doing (132–33). This includes 'selectivity', or the fact that one can have information (or disinformation) specifically tailored to one's own interest or proclivities, 'anonymity', or the degree to which we can communicate anonymously on the Internet, and 'publicity', which refers to the extent to which our lives online have broken down the 'public/private' barrier (chapter 2).

However, I think Cocking and van den Hoven are too quick. While I'm convinced that efficient communication *is* a good tool for the spread of evil online, it's not at all clear to me that those features of our online communities that make them efficient are not also conducive to the spread of good online.[1]

Some Cautionary Remarks

Prior to addressing the good to be found in our online worlds, however, I'd like to take a few paragraphs to critically address what Cocking and van den Hoven perceive as pervasive evils online. While I do not wish to dispute that there are many instances of moral bad that proliferate on the Internet, it's not always clear that the cases cited by Cocking and van den Hoven are representative of our lives online or, indeed, have anything to do with the existence of the Internet per se. For instance, they cite a 2012 incident of a gang rape that was filmed and photographed and subsequently posted online (15). Assuredly evil. But it's hard to see how the Internet itself contributed to the perspective of the perpetrators of the rape, beyond the toxic mixture of young masculinity and alcohol.

Furthermore, while Cocking and van den Hoven correctly note that the Internet—as a medium of extremely efficient communication—allows us to erode the private/public distinction by being considerably freer with our private information, it seems hard to believe that this phenomenon is Internet specific. They write,

> [B]oundary confusions about our public/private lives flourish online. Of particular concern is the vulnerability of our young people to such delusions, and their practice of posting personal details and private

---

1. And while I'm certainly not prepared to do any of this research, it would perhaps be interesting to see whether any *other* technological jumps in the efficiency of communication carried with them similar features that Cocking and van den Hoven identify as problematic. For instance, we might wonder whether the invention of the printing press, moveable type, mass production of newspapers, efficient post delivery, telephone, etc. carried with them some changes, perhaps on a smaller scale, of the sort Cocking and van den Hoven identify as peculiar to the cyber.

information on social networking sites. Again, the usual response is to urge young people to understand their personal information displayed online is not private but often widely publicized. [. . .] While this is plainly good advice so far as it goes, features of the Internet and of how it is used work against seeing things so clearly. [. . .] So while I might be told of the public, rather than private, nature of much Internet interaction, and of the dangers that go with this, I might not see the force of these claims very clearly, if, for example, I am a teenager and my social standing or social inclusion might depend upon divulging personal details and information online. (54)

Once again, while it is certainly true that the Internet has allowed the breakdown of the public/private barrier, especially in young children, to proceed far more efficiently, it would be misleading to say that this is a difference in kind rather than degree. One need only recall the *TigerBeat* pen pal advertisements, in which young people, mostly girls, published their personal information, including their home address, in an internationally distributed teen magazine seeking a pen pal. And while the Internet has clearly provided a great opportunity for young people to trade their personal information for personal connection (real or deceived), the desire to make such a trade is as old as adolescence itself.

Indeed, while Cocking and van den Hoven note a number of horrifying acts that have used the Internet as an instrument or medium of communication, it's not always clear that the Internet is an essential contributor to the evil involved or whether the Internet actually serves as a mediating factor in the subsequent evil. For instance, they note the following case:

When a man in Germany decided to find someone who wanted to be killed and eaten by him, it took only a little while to identify someone, get in touch online, and stage a morbid sexual encounter. We know the details of the case because the perpetrator, Armin Meiwes, videotaped the whole procedure, and was convicted for killing his victim after having eaten his private parts and storing the rest of the body in deep freeze for later consumption. Without the Internet and the dark corners of the deep web hidden from plain sight, it would have been impossible, or at least extremely difficult, to find like-minded people and make these fantasies come true. (42–43)

I do not dispute that without the Internet Armin Meiwes would have had difficulty finding a *willing* victim of his cannibalistic sexual urges. But what is less clear is whether the potential nonexistence of the Internet would have led Meiwes to forego his cannibalism, or simply to find an *un*willing victim.

Furthermore, while there assuredly are a number of websites dedicated to, for example, the promotion of self-harm, anorexia, and, even jihadism, Cocking and van den Hoven do little to convince the reader that these are pervasive aspects of our online lives rather than comparatively small 'corners' of the Internet.[2] Cocking and van den Hoven suggest that there are 500 pro-anorexia sites and also that major jihadist websites take up a large portion of Internet traffic. They write:

> Again (as we suggested earlier in regard to extreme pranks), you might agree that such specific cases depict some terrible corruption, and you might even agree that the online world seems implicated. However, you might well also think that the online worlds of Chesser and the like are very rare, and so a very small part of online activity. And so you might well think that such cases do not really present much of an indictment against life in our online-transformed worlds. Again, none the less, you would be wrong. Sites promoting terror are nothing like marginal dark alleys. As, for example, Barlett reports, the FBI estimates that one of the sites Chesser was involved in belonged to the 1% of sites on the Web that generated the most traffic. (27–28.)

Now this does seem problematic. But the statistic here (i.e., top one percent of sites by Internet traffic) is without context. How many Internet sites are there? Does this mean that they are visited regularly, by a worldwide audience? And, indeed, Cocking and van den Hoven provide ample room for doubt. In discussing the sheer size of the Internet, they write, 'It all started with four connected computers a decade ago. There are now 2.5 billion of them. This makes the Internet the largest manmade artifact. There are a staggering ten to the power of twelve websites (a million million). Every minute there are around a million YouTube views, Google searches and Facebook posts' (34).

Now, this is big. But notice that if there are ten to the power of twelve websites (i.e., a trillion websites), what does it say that any particular site is in the top one percent? Only that it is among the *ten billion most visited websites*. Is this particularly significant? A dark alley? It's unclear, but looked at in this way, it is not immediately obvious that the problems of jihadism, or anorexia advocacy, implicate our lives online *in particular*.

---

2. This is in contrast to the 'pranking' genre of YouTube videos they note, which account for a truly staggering viewership. See Dean Cocking and Jeroen van den Hoven, *Evil Online* (New York: Wiley, 2018) p. 10.

Now, I don't want to argue ahead of myself. I don't want to argue that the efficiency in communication somehow passes by jihadists, pranksters, and those who wish to treat anorexia as a 'lifestyle choice' rather than a debilitating mental illness (17–18). For those with such interests, online tools will provide efficiency in spreading their messages, just as the Internet provides efficient communication or news headlines or the latest *Star Wars* trailer. But what Cocking and van den Hoven have yet to show is that the phenomenon of evil online is pervasive. And what they certainly have so far failed to show is that the phenomenon of *evil* online is pervasive *on balance*—that is, compared to the good that is or can be accomplished given the Internet's power to make communication near costless and near instantaneous. To this I now turn.

The Prosocial and the Promoral

To begin, I'd like to briefly inquire into the nature of what Cocking and van den Hoven call the 'prosocial'. Cocking and van den Hoven often refer to this term in ways that contrast the moral fog of online communities with a manner of development, or set of mental states, that are more aligned with moral norms. However, it is worth distinguishing two different ideas that may be bound up with the idea of a prosocial mindset. The first idea, call this the *prosocial proper*, is a set of mental states that are conducive to or reflective of the social world in which a person finds themselves. To put this another way, it is a mindset that is dedicated to fulfilling general *social* norms—including those set by one's community, family, schools, and so forth.

Let's call the *promoral* a mindset that is generally dedicated to or conducive of the development of moral values, such as a commitment to human flourishing in oneself and others, respect for persons, and so on. Obviously it would be wildly out of place to simply stipulate here what those values are, but for the sake of argument, I'm going to concentrate on human flourishing; generally someone has promoral attitudes when they, for example, display mental dispositions that help to develop such flourishing in themselves and in others around them.

As defined, it should be quite clear that the prosocial and the promoral are distinct. One can be perfectly prosocial but nevertheless quite *anti*moral if one's social norms are themselves not conducive to human flourishing. Indeed, in such circumstances, the promoral may very well be *anti*social. For instance, if one lives in an extremely repressive religious society, it could very well be promoral, but antisocial, to develop an interest in great secular literature. However, in such a case, developing promoral attitudes are to be encouraged, insofar as they contribute to the flourishing of oneself against the prevalent antiflourishing attitudes of one's general social circumstances.

So why is this significant for the present inquiry? I think the answer is this. While I will, at present, accept the general premise that online communities sometimes lead us astray from *prosocial* attitudes, it's not always clear that our lives online lead us astray from prosocial attitudes in a way that is also anti-*moral*. To illustrate this, I'd like to present an episode from the online community Reddit. For those who don't know, Reddit is a massive set of individual 'subreddits', or message boards dedicated to particular topics, anything from discussions about the news of the day, or among enthusiasts of very specific topics (r/synthdiy, for instance, is a dedicated community for those who like to build their own synthesizers), to boards full of silly content (e.g., r/MildlyStartledCats, which includes pictures of, well, you guessed it, and r/ThereWasAnAttempt, which details comical efforts gone wrong) to content that is just plain weird (including r/ImSorryJon, which reimagines the comic strip character Garfield as a grotesque, demented, Arbuckle-tormenting demon), to subreddits that are dedicated to people asking for serious advice on legal, romantic, and other matters. Most posts on Reddit in the latter set of categories involve a question, to which commentators will respond. Those comments are 'upvoted' or 'downvoted' by the other users of Reddit, and upvoting is generally taken to be a sign of approval. The most upvoted comments are displayed first after the original question or post.

The episode I'd like to discuss here is taken from r/relationshipadvice.[3] A young woman was about to get married to her fiancé of eight months. Two days prior to the wedding, the fiancé expressed a desire that the woman submit to a virginity test at the hands of his father and other male members of his extended family. She expressed discomfort at this, but seemed genuinely torn on whether to submit to this humiliating procedure. She summed up her feelings this way: "I want to call off the whole wedding because of this and never talk to him again. But at the same time [it's] only one thing and other than that we are genuinely perfect for each other and I [don't] want to spend my life with anyone else and it is very important to him and his family."

The general Reddit consensus was that this woman should refuse to submit, on the grounds that it is sexual assault and a degrading violation. In short, the morally correct answer. Of course, in the over 12,000 comments on this particular question, there were a number of them that were suspect, displayed 'casual bigotry', or that offered bizarre or borderline insane advice. But those were 'downvoted', and the consensus stood. In a posted update, the young woman declared

---

3. See Reddit, 'Relationship Advice', <https://www.reddit.com/r/relationshipadvice/comments/cx7vro/my22ffiance25mwanthisfathertocheckmy/> [accessed 4 March 2022].

that she refused to submit to the procedure and had ended her relationship with the man who insisted upon it. I submit, a moral win.

I mention this episode as an example of online communities directing someone away from what might have been a pro*social* occurrence (submitting to the social pressure from her fiancé to submit to this sexist and humiliating procedure) to a pro*moral* result, a refusal of this vulnerable young woman to submit to such treatment. Indeed, there are many episodes that have this structure. While Reddit does not have a perfect track record, the advice most commonly upvoted is generally sensible and can be counted on to support, rather than hinder, the flourishing of the advisee. And I think it would be remiss not to say that this is at least in part a result of the fact that this community is online. People in such online communities can ask frank questions that they may otherwise have been ashamed or unempowered to ask given their social communities. But this just illustrates the way in which the fact that our online lives can lead to antisocial outcomes does not entail that these online lives lead to antimoral outcomes. In fact, sometimes the achievement of moral outcomes requires activities that are *not* prosocial proper.

Indeed, one need not look to such dramatic examples to see the ways in which the *anti*social, or at the very least *a*social, nature of some Internet communication can lead specifically to human flourishing. Online communication, especially its worldwide nature, can allow those people who are culturally or geographically isolated a community with which to discuss shared interests, to ask advice, and so on, where doing so might be discouraged.

Good Peculiar to the Online

I've just pointed out one way in which prosocial attitudes and behaviors do not entail promoral attitudes and behaviors, and that in some cases, antisocial attitudes and behaviors, facilitated by the Internet, can lead to moral progress. In this section, I'd like to point out some ways in which those aspects of the Internet Cocking and van den Hoven identify as particularly conducive to evildoing are in fact Janus-faced. Considered fairly, these features can and have been used for the achievement of moral good.

#MeToo

One major complaint that Cocking and van den Hoven have about online environments is the way in which 'the Internet and social media disinhibit people and easily escalate conflicts and problems' (5). However, escalation of this sort is not exclusive to *conflicts and problems* in the way Cocking and van den Hoven seem to suggest. Perhaps the most high-profile instance of this is the by-now-famous #MeToo Movement. In the wake of pervasive sexual harassment and abuse accusations against movie mogul Harvey Weinstein, actor Alyssa Milano, who has a substantial following on the social media platform Twitter, encouraged people to share their own stories of sexual harassment and abuse with the heading '#MeToo' (which had originated with artist and activist Tarana Burke). In the first twenty-four hours of her post, it had generated half a million responses on Twitter and over twelve million posts on the social media platform Facebook. The impact of this social media phenomenon is perhaps immeasurable and in some ways unpredictable. But it has certainly, at the very least, shone a light on pervasive cultures of sexual harassment and abuse in a number of major industries, including entertainment,[4] academia,[5] politics,[6] hospitality,[7] and many others. In addition, the social media campaign has led to companies changing policies for employees and taking a more active role in preventing sexual harassment. While the magnitude of the progress here to be made is as yet to be determined, it is hard to see how the #MeToo movement can be described as anything other than an on-balance good.[8]

In addition, it is hard to see how this on-balance good could have come about without some of the peculiar features of the Internet that make communication so efficient. While the #MeToo movement had been devised as early as 2006,[9] it did not reach its full potential as a force for social change until a popular actor posted on social media. Here the efficiency of online communication was critical. Without the initial tidal wave of support, it is hard to see how the movement would have reached its status as a cultural force for good.

---

4. The most significant cases here involve Weinstein himself and the comedian Louis CK, along with the actor Asia Argento, herself abused by Weinstein but who was accused of sexual assault by a former costar.

5. See, for instance, 'Academia's #MeToo Moment: Women Accuse Professors of Sexual Misconduct', *Washington Post*, 10 May 2018.

6. One need only consult the highly fraught confirmation hearing of now justice Brett Kavanaugh or the high-profile resignation of senator Al Franken.

7. Former restauranteurs John Besh and Mario Batali were both accused of sexual abuse by multiple employees.

8. Of course, this is not to say that it is an unmitigated good. It could be, perhaps, that some individuals have been accused in the wake of the #MeToo movement of sexual harassment in ways that were false, though I am agnostic about whether this has ever occurred in fact.

9. 'Statistics', me too, <https://metoomvmt.org/about/#history> [accessed 26 February 2022].

Deadaptation

And while this next point is a bit a priori, and would need additional empirical study, it seems to me that access to the Internet can be a further force for good when it comes to the phenomenon of adaptive preferences.

Now, I don't have the space here to engage in a philosophical inquiry into the nature of adaptive preferences. This is a fraught issue, but a few things are generally agreed. Adaptive preferences are those that by and large do not reflect the agent's good and are 'adaptations' to the particular limitations a person faces. These adaptations will often result from, for example, a lack of information or a failure to imagine their life in a way different than the one they have.[10]

However, many hold that at least one way to begin to alleviate adaptive preferences (though certainly not a panacea) is exposure to information about the way life might be independent of someone's social circumstances. But to do this properly, one needs an efficient means of communication—one that can allow someone to, perhaps anonymously, explore the (to quote Mill) 'experiments in living' in which others have engaged. The more information available quickly, the more likely it is that someone will not fail to imagine or fail to appreciate how their existence may be different.

Again, this is not a cure-all for problematic adaptive preferences. Some forms of adaptation (what I have elsewhere called 'deep adaptation'[11]) would not be reversed by exposure to the information that the Internet provides. But the fact that the Internet holds great power to alleviate some insidious forms of adaptive preferences is an important good that cannot be ignored.

Collective Play

Having an efficient means of communication means that it is possible to engage in play with a much wider circle of people. And while the possibility of play is

---

10. Cf. Serene Khader, *Adaptive Preferences and Women's Empowerment* (Oxford: Oxford University Press, 2011); Rosa Terlazzo, 'Adaptive Preferences: Merging Political Accounts and Well-Being Accounts', *Canadian Journal of Philosophy*, 45 (2015), 179–96; Martha C. Nussbaum, 'Adaptive Preferences and Women's Options', in *Economics and Philosophy*, 17, 67–88.

11. See, for instance, Dale Dorsey, 'Adaptive Preferences Are a Red Herring', *Journal of the American Philosophical Association*, 3 (2017), 465–84. Note that I have also argued that deep adaptive preferences are more indicative of someone's good than more shallow or surface-level adaptation. If this is correct, it may be that the Internet has at least substantial power to cure the forms of adaptation it would be good to cure.

not, perhaps, the most significant good in our lives, it is one that should not be ignored and is certainly an aspect of any life well-lived.[12]

One important example of our ability to engage each other in collective play is the phenomenon of *rickrolling*. Rickrolling is essentially a broadscale practical joke. The joker sends the mark a hyperlink, ostensibly about something that the mark would find interesting, important, or significant. But rather than redirecting this person to whatever it was the link seemed to offer, they are redirected to YouTube, for the music video of Rick Astley's 'Never Gonna Give You Up'. It's not entirely possible to determine how many times this has occurred, but a superficial view count of this video on YouTube indicates the number is approaching at least a billion.

Now, this is just silly. But it's a kind of collective silliness, a joke that anyone who uses the Internet is in on. But such is the power of a tool of extraordinarily efficient communication. We can engage in silliness, play, and mirth on a *tremendous* scale.

Moral Intensification

Now what do these instances of good tell us? Do they tell us that the Internet is overwhelmingly good? That the instances of evil online, pointed out by Cocking and van den Hoven, are outweighed on balance?

No. Rather, what I think they show is that the Internet is a morally complicated phenomenon. The features of the Internet that make it ripe for a #MeToo movement, also make it ripe for anonymous predation, Internet shaming, and so on. As Cocking and van den Hoven rightly point out, it sometimes has a tendency to give rise to bad behavior on the part of folks who would otherwise not dream of it. However, rather than suggesting that we tend toward evil or good as a result of our lives online, it seems right instead to say that our lives online present a kind of moral intensity that can lead us in many moral directions, with unpredictable results.

By *moral intensity* I mean to refer to an overall increase in the ability of our actions to alter states of affairs, and alter the quality of people's lives, for better *and* worse. Because online communication is so efficient, we have the power to reach massive audiences almost costlessly. And we can use that power for good

---

12. For instance, Martha Nussbaum suggests that play should be included among the ten basic capabilities; see Nussbaum, *Frontiers of Justice* (Cambridge, MA: Harvard University Press, 2007), p. 77.

or ill. Furthermore, acts that may, in isolation, have been harmless monkeyshines can take on a moral life of their own online. For instance, one might post a You-Tube video of a practical joke or prank that would otherwise have been a simple joke between friends, have it 'go viral', and inspire a number of others to engage in behavior that has harmful or even disastrous consequences. One particularly clear example of this phenomenon is the Slender Man. Created as a response to a contest that urged participants to design and post original paranormal drawings, cartoons, and images, the Slender Man (i.e., a very tall shadowy figure) became a viral sensation among connected horror fans, appearing in Internet fiction, forums, and elsewhere. The development of this character became 'open source', with untold numbers of authors and artists posting about the Slender Man in dozens of Internet archives. Five years after the original post, two twelve-year-old girls in Wisconsin stabbed their friend nineteen times, indicating that they were under orders of the Slender Man.

And while our capacity to generate unpredictable bad consequences as a result of our actions online is certainly manifest, unpredictable good consequences multiply as well. A simple retweet requesting victims to tell their stories can give rise to a massive social movement. A simple question from a scared bride-to-be can generate massive awareness of covert sexual assault. A goofy one-off practical joke can lead to billions of instances of collective silliness. Rather than generating amoral fog—though this assuredly happens in some cases—I would instead argue that the prevailing moral phenomenon of the Internet and of our lives online is the *amplification of the consequences*—and the unpredictability of same—of our online activities *given* the efficiency of online communication. The Internet is, in essence, morally intense. And its moral intensity is amplified by its unpredictability.

With its unpredictability, I think, arises two of the great challenges of the Internet. First, a challenge for moral agents. How do we best attempt to control or limit the negative, and promote the good, consequences of our actions in light of the moral intensity of our online world? Second, a challenge for moral theorizing. Given that the consequences of actions are far more unpredictable than we might have originally supposed, is it acceptable to treat such consequences as forming the basis of our inquiry into the moral status of acts? Can we rightfully condemn as *wrong* the original posting of Slender Man? Or praise as *morally exemplary* Alyssa Milano's #MeToo exhortation? And while these questions require substantial reflection, I submit that plausible answers can only be arrived at by looking at the entirety of the Internet's moral intensity and not simply our capacity, real though it is, for great evil online.

☙ JPE ❧

Losing Your Way in the Fog

Reflections on *Evil Online*

PHILIP KITCHER
Columbia University

I

Many philosophers are inclined to dismissive judgments about 'applied ethics'. They think of this line of work as merely requiring straightforward use of ethical principles (the achievements of thinkers who tackle 'fundamental questions') in light of research into the technical details of the pertinent domain. So writing a book about the moral issues posed by the widespread use of the Internet, especially the impact of social media on contemporary lives, ought to be a simple matter. Learn the facts about what is going on, call up your favorite moral theory, and turn the crank.

One of the achievements of *Evil Online* is to provide a decisive refutation of this all-too-common view.[1] To be sure, Dean Cocking and Jeroen van den Hoven offer a parade of appalling stories about life on the World Wide Web. They also show, however, how hard it is to adapt standard ethical categories and principles to comprehend the online behavior that so concerns them. The habits they describe and condemn, often appearing as propensities to staggering cruelty,[2] require the introduction of a new concept: that of 'moral fog'.

What follows will be, in the main, an attempt to develop some of Cocking and van den Hoven's important themes. My principal focus will be on their

---

1. Dean Cocking and Jeroen van den Hoven, *Evil Online* (New York: Wiley, 2018).
2. As with the opening example, describing the hacking of the Epilepsy Foundation of America website, Cocking and van den Hoven, pp. 1–2.

Contact: Philip Kitcher <psk16@columbia.edu>

https://doi.org/10.3998/jpe.2378

conceptual innovation (explicitly motivated by the idea of 'the fog of war'[3]). First, however, I want to consider two independent points.

II

Virtually nobody maintains any more that the Internet is an unmitigated disaster. As Cocking and van den Hoven correctly remark, 'It is no longer an environment where, so far as getting correct answers to questions goes, it could be quite difficult to tell true from false'.[4] Yet their further judgment, hailing the Internet as having 'incredible epistemic power', by enabling people to answer 'just about any' of their questions,[5] needs qualification. Surely, there is a wide range of issues for which a few quick clicks can transform ignorance into true belief (maybe even knowledge?). Despite all the naysayers, Wikipedia has turned out to be an exceptionally valuable resource for those curious about all sorts of things. Or, more exactly, for all those things—and they are legion—about which the experts have achieved consensus *and* that do not threaten the ideas and values of a significant group of people. When either of these conditions lapses, activating a favorite search engine can do more epistemic harm than good. A banal fact of internet life is the invisible hand guiding searchers to sites fitting the profile already constructed for them.[6] Platforms live by the indulgence of advertisers, repaying the largesse by facilitating effective marketing. The pages that appear first on the screen are attuned to the prior history of touring the Web, and the accompanying advertisements harmonize with the interests and preferences attributed to searchers. As an epistemic consequence, a search can all too easily represent only one side of a disputed question, generating the false impression of consensus, where expert agreement has yet to be reached.

Even worse is the fostering and maintenance of controversy on issues that have already been settled, when those issues bear on questions of public policy. An outstanding example is the case of climate change. The reality of anthropogenic global warming has been recognized by climate scientists for well over three decades. Yet, even today, many Internet sites challenge the expert consensus, offering apparently 'scientific' graphs and figures to trace an alternative history of the Earth's mean temperature.[7] Slick videos contest the research, and

---

3. Cocking and van den Hoven, p. 86.

4. Cocking and van der Hoven, p. 40.

5. Cocking and van der Hoven, p. 40.

6. See Nicola Mössner and Philip Kitcher, 'Knowledge, Democracy, and the Internet', *Minerva*, 55 (2017), pp. 1–24.

7. See Philip Kitcher and Evelyn Fox Keller, *The Seasons Alter* (New York: Norton/Liveright 2017), especially chapter 1.

even the honesty, of leading climate scientists. The result is a mass of misinformation that has surely retarded action to combat a threat as severe as any our species has faced in its recorded history.

During the years since the advent of cable news, political divisions have fragmented the news media. In turn, the fragmentation has intensified the divisions. The vicious spiral has been accelerated by the Internet, with the consequence of making policy debates ever more contentious and difficult to resolve. Democracy relies on an informed citizenry, able to align voting preferences with genuine interests. When confusion is sown, and when an alleged source of knowledge partitions the electorate, democracy's claim to promote the freedom of the people is undermined. Citizens troop to the polls, and, 'instructed' in part by what they have read online, select candidates whose policies are at odds with their most central goals and aspirations. In the act supposed to express their freedom, they defeat what they most want to achieve. It is one of the great ironies of our times.

Cocking and van den Hoven's book is largely concerned with the dark side of the internet. Their wish to register some awareness of the epistemic benefits it has brought is easy to understand. Yet here, too, the large costs should be noted. What does it profit a species to gain the entire wisdom of Wikipedia and lose both the best (or least bad?) form of government and its planet as well?

III

Cocking and van den Hoven explore episodes and patterns of behavior whose pathologies are so striking as to silence any objections about the aptness of their title. 'Evil' is notoriously difficult to define, and, wisely, they don't venture a definition. As with obscenity, we know it when we see it, and we are shown it again and again throughout their discussions. Evil actions are often seen as extreme instances of moral badness. Nevertheless, for all the repugnance and even horror they arouse, they may not be the most significant wrongs committed in the online world.

Should those who design and write for sites disseminating disinformation relevant to major policy issues be included among the evildoers? They are certainly less flamboyant than the characters who star in Cocking and van den Hoven's horror stories. Yet the damage they do to human lives may be orders of magnitude greater than that perpetrated by the cyberbullies, not only in extent but also in intensity. Purveyors of 'alternative realities' today may open the path to the autocracies of tomorrow; the 'enemies of the people' rounded up by future dictators to be imprisoned and tortured may be connected by a long causal process to people who sowed Internet deceit in the interests of short-term political gain. The 'merchants of doubt'[8] whose desires to maintain the profits derived from fossil fuels lead them to spread confusion on the Web are likely to retard action to address climate change; the costs of their contributions will be measured in future deaths, from starvation, drought, fire, flood, and (possibly agonizing) pandemics. What these malefactors do isn't obviously evil, at least not in any everyday sense. Given the high stakes, however, it should surely be a matter of moral concern.

An obvious reply: misconduct of the types just considered is importantly different from Cocking and van den Hoven's central focus. The turpitude of the actors is only contingently connected with the online world. The internet simply serves them as a useful means for implementing their designs. Fair enough. Nevertheless, there are aspects of Internet life Cocking and van den Hoven (rightly) consider, that share the potential for huge damage to human lives and to human society. In various passages, they are sensitive to the ways in which the increasing prominence—even dominance—of 'screens' in daily life affects social relations and the development of children.[9] Much of their discussion connects to the forms of online conduct on which they mostly focus. My own worries are more general. Even when there are no obvious pathologies, lives spent largely online threaten important values. They may bring about stunted and impoverished forms of human existence.

It's commonplace, fully appreciated by Cocking and van den Hoven, that Facebook and its ilk have modified our concept of friendship. As they rightly point out, when people measure themselves by the number of their 'friends', the quality and depth of individual friendships is likely to decrease.[10] Moreover, the pressure to fashion the most positive image of oneself, thus improving one's 'statistics' is a distortion of autonomous development.[11] Cocking and van den Hoven are somewhat reassured by the overlap between online and offline social connections.[12] All these are important points and deserve emphasis. I wonder, though, whether they go far enough.

Friendships vary in closeness and in the depth of mutual understanding.[13] Because our time is limited, multiplying the number of friends we have diminishes the amount of time—and attention—we can devote to each of them. Of course, the limited resource, time-spent-with-X, might be apportioned unequally.

---

8. See Naomi Oreskes and Erik Conway, *Merchants of Doubt* (New York: Bloomsbury, 2010).
9. Cocking and van der Hoven, *Evil Online*, pp. 41, 50, 75–77, and 78.
10. Cocking and van der Hoven, p. 76.
11. Cocking and van der Hoven, pp. 75 and 78.
12. Cocking and van der Hoven, p. 78.
13. For a sensitive philosophical discussion of friendship, from which I have learned much, see Alexander Nehamas, *On Friendship* (New York: Basic Books, 2016).

A large number of superficial friendships could coexist with a small number of relationships achieving the depth and intimacy realized in the bonds we most admire. Whether that occurs for any large proportion of those for whom life is infused with hours spent on social media is a matter for sociological research. Assuming, however, that many people now enter into friendships more diluted—thinner—than those central to the lives of the past, the consequence is likely to be registered in new standards and norms of human relationships. At a time when many reflective people are worried about the ways in which conceptions of living well are often dominated by consumerism—'He who dies with the most toys wins'—the abandonment of intimacy with its rewards and its often stringent demands would be an enormous loss.

The metaphorphosis I fear might occur without any of the pathologies Cocking and van den Hoven focus on. Imagine a world in which the proportion of the day spent online continues to increase. Suppose the internet becomes as safe and well-mannered as you like. Cyberbullying, sexual predation, revenge porn, cruel pranks all become things of the past. Yet the pressure to advertise oneself positively on social media remains, and even intensifies. When pretenders are unmasked, they are not humiliated or publicly scorned. The offenses are noted. Reprimands are administered firmly but with restraint. Liars lose friends by the score and, because worth is measured by the sheer number of 'friends', the punishment is felt.

In this envisaged world, people connected on the internet still sometimes interact offline. Because of the hours they devote to social media, the interactions are typically less frequent and shorter than those through which friendships of the kinds most admired are developed and sustained. Most importantly, some *dimensions* of friendship become rarer. The spate of online chat doesn't offer much opportunity for serious exploration of goals, for thinking through uncertain prospects together, for providing and receiving aid or consolation, for sharing the deepest joys. When an intimate friendship has already been formed, contact online can provide resources for maintaining it (although it may still require occasions on which friends can talk face to face or act in a joint project). What strikes me as less clear is how multidimensional intimacy is achieved without shared experiences, without episodes of standing together against some common threat, without the moments when troubles are confessed and advice is sought. The world I have imagined has banished online evil. Despite that, it is a world in which one of the most valuable aspects of human life has been reduced and cheapened.

New technologies have frequently invited jeremiads. In an older generation, concerned parents often worried about the effects of television on their children's development. So, it is reasonable to reply to my concerns by charging me with repeating a familiar Luddite complaint. There's no evidential basis for supposing the future I've imagined to have any large probability. Nonetheless, it is surely a possibility, one that should arouse concern. Discussions of the damage wrought by the internet should not be restricted to the manifest evils. Vigilance about more subtle and insidious ways of making the world worse is, I suggest, a good idea.

IV

At the heart of Cocking and van den Hoven's project is a cluster of related questions. How does it happen that, placed in an online environment, some people—not obviously 'bad people'—do appalling things? What has caused them to deviate from their normal, morally acceptable, patterns of conduct? How does our understanding of morality and of the moral training of the young need to be expanded to reduce the frequency with which the pathologies occur?

Cocking and van den Hoven approach these issues by proposing that the evildoers are in a moral fog. Their moral education has instilled into them habits of action and reflection able to guide them correctly under many of the conditions they experience. In front of their screens, however, something goes wrong. The fog descends. They lose their compass and their way. And they do appalling things.

These strike me as good questions, and I am sympathetic to Cocking and van den Hoven's approach to them. Much of what they say is insightful. Yet, as they are surely aware, the notion of a moral fog is itself—well—foggy. In what follows, I shall try to suggest a different way of articulating their problem and of developing techniques for addressing their questions. My reformulation of their central themes already hints at the character of my alternative. Where they emphasize the fog, I consider the compass.

Compasses can fail to guide for all sorts of reasons. They may be mislaid, or unreadable in the available light, or damaged, or useless because one doesn't know which of the points marks their destination or because they are affected by the presence of a sufficiently strong magnet—or one may simply not see how to proceed in the indicated direction. Switching metaphors from fog to compass opens up the possibility of viewing what initially appears as a unified phenomenon as covering a range of different cases. I'll exploit that possibility.

A good place to start is with a philosophical debate about which Cocking and van den Hoven write with admirable cogency and clarity. The rich history of discussion of how apparently good (normal, law-abiding) people can commit evils has raised questions about whether it is apt to ascribe a standing character to a person and thus whether talking of people as 'good people' or 'bad people' makes sense. Cocking and van den Hoven's review of work in social psychology is well-informed and accurate. One important source doesn't figure in it: the joint work of Walter Mischel, Yuichi Shoda, and Rodolfo Mendoza-Denton.[14] The study I have in mind was a follow-up to Mischel's earlier research, in which he had amassed considerable evidence for situationism (the thesis that conduct varies in important ways with the surrounding circumstances). That earlier conclusion was further confirmed by Mischel and his coauthors. Observing behavior at a summer camp, they recorded how traits like *being outgoing* and *being willing to take risks* varied across contexts. But they were also able to show how individuals had distinctive profiles. When placed in situations of one kind, a child would be deferential; in the rest of the observed circumstances, deference vanished. Their research questioned the oversimple way in which we use vocabulary to discuss character. We assume people to have stable characters in being disposed to exhibit a particular type of behavior across the board: the brave person will act bravely, come what may. Our actual character traits are more complex, consisting in a spectrum of behavioral responses keyed to different classes of situations.

Following Mischel, Shoda, and Mendoza-Denton, let's think of moral training (considered as something that occurs not only in youth but throughout a lifetime) as setting up, at any given point in a person's existence, a complex of dispositions. Some of these dispositions are *habits of action*. Much of our conduct occurs without reflection. People often don't ask themselves whether to wave to an acquaintance, or if they should step back to let someone pass by, or whether they should head off to work in the morning. With respect to these and myriad other parts of our conduct, we frequently don't wonder if what we are doing is permissible. We simply do it.

Of course, there are occasions on which we do stop to think, when some feature of the context triggers another disposition—a morally crucial disposition—that suspends the habit of action and calls on us to take stock. As Bernard Williams famously argued, it's a mistake to suppose reflection always to be justified.[15] The husband who engages in moral inquiry before plunging in to save his drowning wife has had 'one thought too many'. Indeed, as Shakespeare taught us in *Hamlet*, people can have *many* thoughts too many. An ideally trained moral agent would be disposed to moral meditation in all and only the situations for which the proper course is unclear, leaving habit to operate unchecked in each of the rest. Much of everyday moral education consists in equipping the young with the habits society has approved, freeing the growing moral agent to work things through on the occasions on which matters are confused.

---

14. 'Situation-Behavior Profiles as a Locus of Consistency in Personality', *Current Directions in Psychological Science*, 11, no. 2 (2002), pp. 50–54.

15. Bernard Williams, 'Persons, Character, and Morality', in *Moral Luck* (Cambridge: Cambridge University Press, 1981).

Among the habits also required are those put to work in moral reflection. It isn't enough to be aptly disposed to pause or to let habit generate action. Besides knowing *when* to reflect, one also has to know *how*. According to many influential views of moral life, this know-how is largely (even completely) reducible to a system of moral principles. When a problematic situation has caused one to stop and think, they consult their corpus of precepts, find the one that fits the circumstances, determine what it counsels them to do on this occasion, and then they follow that advice. Views like this lay at the root of the 'turn-the-crank' conception of applied ethics with which I began. (Perhaps I caricature—but many discussions of biomedical ethics, environmental ethics, and business ethics seem to adopt this kind of simplistic picture.)

In any number of taxing moral predicaments, recommending this type of procedure is hopeless. We can't find any precept fitting the case at hand, or we don't understand the moral dimensions of the circumstances well enough to decide which of several potential principles best suits it, or there are several principles judged to be applicable and they pull in contrary directions.[16] What we have explicitly been taught doesn't seem to help. Nor, when we try to find analogies with other situations, whether they are real instances we have experienced or historical cases that have been thoroughly analyzed, or fictitious examples we or others have constructed, do we take them to resolve our quandary. The moral propositions we believe don't apply themselves.

Moral philosophy is often beguiled by a faulty analogy with natural science. The complete moral theory is supposed to be akin to the picture Newton (and many scientists—and even more fans of science—after him) envisaged for the complete system of the world. There will be a small number of fundamental principles (of extraordinary generality) from which any correct moral statement can be derived by inserting the pertinent boundary and initial conditions. The subsequent history of the natural sciences has belied the Newtonian dream.[17] Yet, even if it had been sustained, the daily *practice* of the sciences is remarkable for the common difficulty of bringing high theory to bear on the local situation. As Thomas Kuhn pointed out, anyone who has ever learned any significant amount of any science encounters a recurrent phenomenon: the chapter presents a small number of new principles; the student understands those principles, committing them firmly to memory; but, faced with the exercises at the end, the mind goes completely blank.[18]

---

16. Dewey offers a cogent statement of the difficulty. See *Human Nature and Conduct*, in *The Middle Works*, vol. 14 (Carbondale: Southern Illinois University Press, 1988), p. 74.

17. See John Dupré, *The Disorder of Things* (Cambridge, MA: Harvard University Press, 1993); and Nancy Cartwright, *The Dappled World* (Cambridge: Cambridge University Press, 1999).

18. T. S. Kuhn, *The Structure of Scientific Revolutions* (Chicago: University of Chicago Press, 1962).

Contemporary accounts of scientific practice emphasize the skills, acquired in training and subsequently put to work. Much of the professional's knowledge is tacit. Why should moral practice be different? Instead of thinking of moral training as simply presenting a list of moral principles and as disciplining the will to follow the propositions engraved on consciousness by proper education, conceive it as delivering a set of dispositions. These dispositions—*sensitivities* to give them a name—guide moral agents as they encounter new situations.

The basic sensitivity distinguishes those contexts in which action-guiding habits are allowed to proceed from those triggering a need for reflection. Probably none of us has a perfect version of this sensitivity. We go wrong in two main ways, either by plunging ahead when we should stop to reflect or by dithering when we ought to act decisively. (The contrast is encapsulated in two familiar proverbs, whose opposition brings out the failure of the morality-as-a-system-of-principles view: 'Look before you leap!' and 'He who hesitates is lost'.) Within these two large classes of potential errors, we have our own individual propensities to go astray. For each of us, there is a set of contexts in which we mistakenly let habit prevail when we should pause to reflect, as well as a set of circumstances in which we wrongly inhibit our customary behavior.[19] The two sets define a personal profile, a complex example of the kinds of profiles studied by Mischel, Shoda, and Mendoza-Denton. These profiles connect directly to the questions raised by Cocking and van den Hoven: Is it common for internet users either to follow habits where they ought to stop and think or to suspend habits of everyday consideration for others after engaging in morally distorted musings, reassuring themselves of the permissibility of behavior they would otherwise firmly reject?

The latter question raises issues about the derivative sensitivities our moral training instills in us. Mapping those sensitivities, and recognizing the general form of the associated personal profiles, requires an understanding of the methodology of moral inquiry. Elsewhere, I have offered some proposals about proper methods of moral inquiry.[20] On the view I suggest, moral inquiry is primarily social. Societies make moral progress through identifying problems with the currently accepted moral framework and solving (more exactly: partially solving) those problems. A satisfactory moral methodology must answer two

---

19. I'm inclined to speculate that, for the vast majority of people, the principal deficiency is thoughtlessness, the tendency to charge ahead when reflection is required. It also seems likely that this type of mistake causes greater moral harm. But these conjectures call for serious empirical research. So far as I know, nobody has yet done it.

20. For an early version, see Philip Kitcher, *The Ethical Project* (Cambridge, MA: Harvard University Press, 2011), chapter 9. My thoughts about moral methodology are more systematically developed in *Moral Progress* (New York: Oxford University Press, 2021).

main questions: How are problems discerned? And, How are they then properly addressed? For the sake of simplicity, I'll focus here on one particular way of recognizing problems and of tackling them.[21]

Historically, moral advances have been slow, messy, and vulnerable to many contingent factors. (The movement to abolish slavery, the fight for greater opportunities for women, and the overcoming of homophobia testify to these features of progressive transitions.) They have often been initiated when the sufferings of a conventionally marginalized group become a matter for wider discussion. William James was far too optimistic in declaring that if the philosopher 'makes a bad mistake the cries of the wounded will soon inform him of the fact'.[22] Sometimes, however, the cries of the wounded do arouse sufficient social concern to spark a debate and, usually after long and bloody struggles, most members of the relevant society are prepared to admit that a mistake has been made. When moral methodology focuses on such episodes, the task is to recognize the ways in which successful resolution was eventually achieved and to propose a procedure for moral inquiry capable of streamlining the process.

As I have argued, human moral life has a long history, measured in tens of thousands of years.[23] It results from a central problem in the human condition: our need to live in societies mixed by age and sex while still lacking a full psychological capacity for responding to our fellows. We are able on occasion to recognize the goals and aspirations of others and to modify our own actions so that they harmonize. Yet this ability frequently breaks down, and we thwart the intentions of people with whom we causally interact. The moral project amplifies our responsiveness. The shortcomings of our evolved psychology are partially remedied by the social working out of accepted patterns of conduct.

The major historical examples of moral progress reveal how this can occur. What is needed is the clear representation of the ways in which hitherto accepted practices bear on the lives of different classes of people, followed by a sympathetic response to the various perspectives and predicaments. In principle, that can be done without fighting a civil war, or campaigning against monstrous 'men-women', or stoning gays. Identify moral problems by taking the protests that arise seriously enough to investigate them; conduct the investigation by assembling a body inclusive enough to represent all those who are causally affected; let that body deliberate, using only information well-supported by the

---

21. *Moral Progress* distinguishes two generic cases: problems of exclusion and problems of false consciousness. Here, I shall only consider the former.

22. William James, 'The Moral Philosopher and the Moral Life', in *The Will to Believe and Other Essays in Popular Philosophy* (Cambridge MA: Harvard University Press, 1979), p. 158.

23. See Kitcher, *The Ethical Project*.

available evidence and committed to finding a conclusion all can live with. If the verdict takes the complaint to be justified, expand the body by including representatives of all groups potentially affected by the various options for amending the status quo. Let this new panel of deliberators discuss further, until they can arrive at a modification all can tolerate.[24]

How does that social method help the individual? How should each of us proceed when the moral resources acquired in our development seem inadequate to the current situation? None of us can snap our fingers and assemble appropriately constituted advisory boards to counsel us. What we can manage, however, is a simulation of how we imagine a properly conducted social inquiry would go. The adequacy of our imaginative attempt will depend on a number of sensitivities. First, our ability to discern the range of options available to us. Second, an ability to identify the kinds of people who would be affected by each of the alternatives. Third, an understanding of their various perspectives. Fourth, some sense of how they might respond to one another's needs and aspirations, if they were firmly committed to leaving nobody unsatisfied. The first two of these sensitivities are primarily cognitive, depending on talents for recognizing causal structure. The third and fourth introduce affective dimensions, requiring skills in empathizing with the viewpoints and circumstances of others.

An adequate moral psychology would analyze the four sensitivities into more basic elements, thus enabling empirical investigations of the kinds of profiles individuals (and groups) come to have. Even in advance of a more sophisticated account, it's possible to extend Cocking and van den Hoven's picture of moral fog by differentiating a number of ways in which an internet user's moral compass may break down. As already noted, one class of instances of online evil may come about through thoughtlessness: seated at the computer, the wrongdoer just follows impulse or habit, without pausing to examine their conduct. Others check their behavior. They ask if what they were going to do is OK—and, after some thought, they decide to go ahead. Although they have engaged in moral inquiry, it has gone badly.

The trouble may occur in any number of ways. Here are some principal varieties.

(1) Choosing the wrong class of "deliberators": instead of focusing on those affected, people consider the opinions of their friends, gaining reassurance from the thought that 'everyone does it'.

---

24. This paragraph compresses an approach I defend at length in *Moral Progress*. Many qualifications and nuances have been omitted. But I hope a rough précis provides enough to explain my version of the methodological project.

(2) Misrepresenting the impact on others: adverse effects on particular people are minimized; 'it's just a prank (they should be able to take a joke)'.

(3) Failure to represent the situation of others or to empathize with it: this may occur as a general insensitivity to others' feelings or as hostility toward members of a particular group ('they deserve it—they're losers'[25]).

(4) Overestimation of the value expressed in the action: while a negative impact on some others is acknowledged, it is seen as outweighed ('the whole point of the web is to let people feel free to be themselves').

There are surely other scenarios, and those I've briefly noted can combine and interact. A moral compass—like its everyday namesake—can let the user down for all sorts of reasons. Even if the prankster, the cyberbully, the poster of revenge porn, and the cruel hacker are all lost in moral fog, it would be useful to understand the various processes through which they have lost their way.

V

Useful because understanding the different etiologies might help decrease the incidence of online evil. If my general approach to moral life is right, moral training is always likely to be incomplete. Societies discover methods to educate their members so that most of them have sensitivities adapted to most of the circumstances they encounter. Moral mistakes occur most frequently when the situation poses a novel challenge. Unprepared for this type of context, the agent's acquired resources prove inadequate. Online evil results from a spectacular change in the frequency with which the previously cultivated sensitivities are not up to the job—at least for a significant number of people. What we would like to do is to reform moral education so that fewer Internet users engage in the practices Cocking and van den Hoven so powerfully describe. That requires (in my view) recognizing the sensitivities needed for success in moral navigation of the internet world and devising educational programs for instilling them. (Although we shouldn't expect any such program to anticipate future technological changes and the new predicaments they generate.)

---

25. This is the best rationalization I can come up with for the case of the people who hacked into the Epilepsy Help site. But perhaps this judgment reflects the limits of my own moral imagination.

Why do good people do appalling things? The question arose in response to the behavior of ordinary citizens under Nazism and it was intensified by Milgram's notorious experiments. Cocking and van den Hoven reasonably devote space to considering the ensuing discussion. In the end, however, it seems to me right to abandon the question. People are variously sensitive. Internet usage exposes differences we might previously not have suspected. Individuals whose moral status is indistinguishable outside their time at the keyboard are sharply differentiated by what they do online. In contexts beyond those considered in their early training, some are better able to appreciate causal impact, better at imagining the reactions of the affected groups, more empathetic, and so forth. So far as we fix the class of challenging situations by including just those currently experienced, they turn out to be better people. If we concentrated on the predicaments encountered in the world in which they grew up, that judgment would not hold. And—who knows?—in some range of environments arising in their future, they might turn out to be worse. If blame has a role in responding to the online evildoers, it should be by teaching them—and others potentially like them—how to do better.

I hope it is clear how dismissive judgments of applied ethics are completely wrongheaded. As the world changes, our species constantly needs adjustments of its moral practices to keep pace. *Online Evil* begins an important enterprise, that of understanding how the sensitivities of ordinary people are often morally inadequate in a world transformed by internet technology. We should all be grateful to Cocking and van den Hoven for having initiated a crucial project in moral and educational reform.

♠JPE♠

Self-Presentation and Privacy Online

CARISSA VÉLIZ
University of Oxford

Keywords: privacy, self-presentation, rights, right to privacy, surveillance, influencers, digital ethics, ai ethics.

In their book *Evil Online*, Dean Cocking and Jeroen van den Hoven argue that a collection of characteristics of the online world have created 'a moral fog' that corrupts people's moral compass.[1] One of those problematic characteristics, they argue, is the ability to self-present online largely on one's own terms. In the offline world, we have access to people's identities in a richness that partly lies beyond people's control. For instance, we may want to present a calm version of ourselves, but our biting our nails might betray our feelings of anxiety. That plurality of the self allows other people the opportunity to be better informed about who we are, and to partly construct and support our identity. Cocking and van den Hoven argue that, by acting in a way that does not openly acknowledge our anxiety, but that can attend to it by calming us down, others can promote our autonomy and privacy.

In this paper, I critically assess this stance and others like it. In section 1, I analyze the relationship between control over self-presentation and privacy and argue that, while they are both tightly connected, they are not one and the same thing. Distinguishing between control over self-presentation and privacy has important practical implications for the online world. In section 2, I investigate self-presentation online and argue that, while there might be an illusion that one can self-present on one's own terms online, that mirage often reveals itself as

---

1. Dean Cocking and Jeroen van den Hoven, *Evil Online* (New York: Wiley, 2018).

Contact: Carissa Véliz <carissa.veliz@philosophy.ox.ac.uk>
  https://orcid.org/0000-0002-3189-3994

https://doi.org/10.3998/jpe.2379

unrealistic because of external and internal constraints. I further argue that what is most noteworthy about self-presentation online, in contrast to self-presentation offline, is the pressure to be on display at all times. In section 3, I argue that to combat some of the negative trends we are witnessing online we need, on the one hand, to cultivate a culture of privacy, in contrast to a culture of exposure. On the other hand, we need to readjust how we understand self-presentation online. I argue that in some cases we should understand it in similar terms to how we understand advertisement or fiction. By changing our conventions online, we would be taking away some of people's control over self-presentation by not taking their online personae at face value.

I.   Self-Presentation and Privacy

Cocking and van den Hoven join a long tradition of philosophers and thinkers who have rightly pointed out that self-presentation is intimately related to privacy. How close that relationship is, however, is less clear, and how we conceptualize it has important implications for how we should shape social media in order to combat negative trends online. In what follows, I will assess the relationship between self-presentation and privacy and argue that, although connected, they are not one and the same.

In *The Presentation of Self in Everyday Life*, the sociologist Ervin Goffman described the many ways in which human beings put up certain performances for each other, depending on the audience and context. In public, we tend to put forth our best sides. We dress up nicely, try to behave politely, and do our best to look the way we want others to perceive us. We conceal from our intended audiences the 'dirty work': going to the bathroom, tidying up, and all the preparation that it takes to show ourselves in the best possible light. We show our strengths and hide our weaknesses.[2]

Because everyone has an interest in self-presentation, we help each other keep up appearances by dividing spaces and situations into front- and backstages and through norms of etiquette. In a restaurant, for instance, the front area are the tables, while the backstage, where waiters can relax their performance, is the kitchen. If we see someone making a mistake that could embarrass them, we make an effort to look away, smooth things over, or steer people's attention elsewhere. When we walk down the street, it is tactful to practice what

---

2. Erving Goffman, *The Presentation of the Self in Everyday Life* (New York: Anchor, 1959).

Goffman calls 'civic inattention'—do not stare, follow people around, or photo-graph them, to name a few norms.[3]

Self-presentation is closely related to privacy. According to James Rachels, the value of privacy relies on the 'connection between our ability to control who has access to us and to information about us, and our ability to create and maintain different sorts of social relationships with different people'.[4] You are bound to behave differently with your students than with your spouse—and all parties are probably grateful for that. Privacy helps us keep different kinds of relationships. If we lived in a completely transparent society, with no front- and backstage, it would be harder to play different roles in different settings with different people.

More recently, Andrei Marmor has argued that 'the underlying interest pro-tected by the right to privacy is the interest in having a reasonable measure of control over ways you present yourself to others'.[5] Rachels and Marmor agree that our interest in self-presentation underlies our right to privacy. Rachels, however, writes that self-presentation is 'one of the most important reasons why we value privacy',[6] suggesting that there might be other reasons as well. Marmor seems to think that self-presentation is the *only* interest underlying our right to privacy.

Since we need a reasonably predictable environment regarding the flow of information to successfully control our self-presentation, a violation of the right to privacy, then, for Marmor, 'consists in the manipulation of the environment in ways that unjustifiably diminish one's ability to control how one presents oneself to others'.[7]

Cocking and van den Hoven do not give an explicit account of the relation-ship between self-presentation and privacy. They do, however, emphasize the close connection between the two, and give some examples that can serve as the basis for further analysis. They imagine a situation in which one is out with a friend of theirs and she encounters her ex, who is with his new lover:

> The presentation of less chosen aspects of our selves often also provide the object for the expression of certain relational aspects of respect for one another's privacy. For the purpose of respecting the legitimate claim of people to keep some of their thoughts and feelings to themselves, and to have some choice and control over the 'self' they present to us

---

3. Erving Goffman, *Behavior in Public Places* (New York: Free Press, 1963), pp. 24 and 84.

4. James Rachels, 'Why Privacy Is Important', *Philosophy and Public Affairs*, 4, no. 4 (1975), p. 326.

5. Andrei Marmor, 'What Is the Right to Privacy?', *Philosophy and Public Affairs*, 43, no. 1 (2015), p. 22.

6. Marmor, 'What Is the Right', p. 329.

7. Marmor, 'What Is the Right', p. 25.

for public engagement or scrutiny, we can—and often should—choose not to address what their conflicting, less chosen and controlled, self-presentations might tell us. My friend's ex-partner, for instance, may no longer presume to engage in the private concerns of my friend, and so her anxiety and discomfort [when they] encounter, while recognized, need not be addressed and subjected to his unwelcome attention. This is one way then, in which relational aspects of our respect for the privacy of others can be shown.[8]

Cocking and van den Hoven consider other similar examples to the same effect. If we have a work colleague who, we can see, is bitter and unhappy (even if he does not 'give' us this information, he 'gives it off'), 'we may respect his privacy and autonomy by not remarking on this misery and ill-will publicly and explicitly'.[9]

Given these remarks and examples, it seems like Cocking and van den Hoven are equating control over self-presentation and privacy, much like Marmor. As long as we support and do not interfere with people's self-presentation, we are respecting their privacy.

My own view is closer to Rachels than to Cocking and van den Hoven or Marmor. The ability to self-present is one of the elements why we value privacy, but it does not amount to privacy, and thinking it does will mislead us into misguided practical implications.

To see how control over self-presentation and privacy are not one and the same thing, it is helpful to analyze them in terms of necessary and sufficient conditions. In some cases, one can have control over self-presentation and no privacy, which shows that privacy is not necessary for control over self-presentation. If you have a good relationship with your spouse, you may be able to perform different roles in their presence, therefore having control over self-presentation, but no privacy (with respect to your spouse). Your spouse, then, may know what you look like first thing in the morning. They might have seen you at your very worst. But that does not impede your ability to act like a professional in front of them (e.g., giving a public talk or bumping into your boss and playing the role you play at work). That your partner knows how you are in very different roles and contexts—in the morning, at your worst, with your boss, and, say at a party—makes you have less privacy with respect to them than you do with respect to other people, but it does not necessarily impede your self-presentation. Privacy, then, is not always necessary for control over self-presentation.

---

8. Cocking and van den Hoven, *Evil Online*, pp. 63–64.
9. Cocking and van den Hoven, p. 71.

A critic might want to argue that your control over your self-presentation is jeopardized in front of your spouse. Your spouse, after all, could interrupt your performance to describe to others what you look like in the morning. It is not clear that such a violation of the right to privacy would interfere with your self-presentation. Suppose you are giving an important talk in front of an audience of strangers at an international conference. If you suddenly learned that you forgot to close the curtains of your room at the hotel where you are all staying, and all of those people had seen you as you woke up and got ready for the talk, you might feel so mortified that it might impede your capacity to perform. In that case, a loss of privacy interferes with the capacity to self-present as a slick professional. But if it is your spouse who tries to tell them that you do not always look this slick, or tries to show them a picture of a dishevelled version of you, they would be embarrassing themselves by flouting social norms of decorum. In that case, it seems that your partner's self-presentation is compromised, not so much yours. If your self-presentation is affected, it is as a result of your partner acting in an embarrassing way (that is, their being your partner might reflect badly on you).[10]

Part of why we care about self-presentation is because it says something about our competence and values. If someone does not show up dressed appropriately to an important work meeting, either they do not care enough about the meeting or they are incapable of keeping up their self-presentation, which introduces doubts about their competence as a professional and their self-control.

This insight is relevant to the relationship between privacy and self-presentation. If a performance such as a talk is ruined because of a failure of self-presentation, people are more likely to negatively judge and embarrass the presenter. If the talk goes badly because the presenter woke up too late and did not have time to clean up, then that will reflect badly on them. But if the performance is interrupted because of someone else trying to undermine the presenter, the shame may be on them. That will not be true in every case, of course—sometimes people succeed in undermining one another. One counterexample is enough, however, to show that privacy is not necessary for control over self-presentation.

There are other examples, however. Imagine you become interesting to an intelligence agency. Spies begin to follow you around, they put microphones in your house and listen to your conversations, record your online activity, and so on. It might be the case that they are spying on you in order to get to someone else—say, unbeknownst to you, your cousin, with whom you live, is a suspected

---

10. On 'dramaturgical discipline' and self-control, see Goffman, *The Presentation of the Self*, chapter 6.

criminal. The spies do not interfere with your self-presentation in the slightest, and they have no plans to disseminate your private information, as they are after your cousin, not you. But that you have lost privacy by being heavily spied on seems clear.[11]

So much for privacy not being necessary for control over self-presentation. On the other side of the coin, control over self-presentation is not necessary for privacy. We can imagine someone being forced to dress in a certain way (e.g., formal attire for work), thereby affecting their control over self-presentation without this action having any effect on their privacy.[12]

Privacy is not sufficient for control over self-presentation either. Suppose you want to self-present as a slick professional to someone you think is watching you at a work party. And imagine that you fail to self-present yourself as a slick professional because you are too tired, or anxious, or drunk to pull it off. That failure of self-presentation can have negative effects on your self-esteem, for instance, but it need not correlate with a loss of privacy. Perhaps your intended audience did not even notice your presence and therefore your failure to self-present—maybe they were distracted, or too drunk, or blind. Your privacy is therefore intact with respect to your intended audience, since they did not see you, but you still failed to self-present like the slick professional you wanted to appear like.

Similarly, control over self-presentation is not sufficient for privacy. When you talk about intimate matters with a friend, you are (voluntarily) losing privacy while retaining control over your self-presentation.

In short, privacy often supports control over self-presentation, but it is neither necessary nor sufficient for successful self-presentation. Likewise, control over self-presentation often supports privacy, but is neither necessary nor sufficient for privacy. The distinction matters—especially in the digital age. If we do not recognize that privacy interests go beyond self-presentation interests, we will be led to think that surveillance capitalism—the constant data collection and analysis carried out by corporate and governmental institutions for the purposes of social control and profit—does not impact our privacy, because it often does not have a direct impact on our capacity to self-present.

As I argue elsewhere, privacy is the quality of having one's personal information and 'sensorial space' unaccessed. You have privacy with respect to a certain person to the extent that that person does not know anything personal about

---

11. Someone like Marmor, however, would be forced to argue that having an intelligence agency spy on someone is not a matter of privacy. Such a stance may be consistent with his theory, but it is completely at odds with common-sense understandings of privacy.

12. Björn Lundgren, 'A Dilemma for Privacy as Control', *Journal of Ethics*, 24 (2020), pp. 165–75.

you, and to the extent they cannot see, hear, or touch you in contexts in which people do not commonly want to be the object of others' attention.[13]

Let us go back to Cocking and van den Hoven's offline privacy examples. When, in a social setting, you catch a glimpse of someone's involuntary and revealing gestures that betray some feeling they wish to hide, and you act with discretion, thereby supporting the person's self-presentation and autonomy, you save their blushes, but you are not protecting their privacy. Therefore, when a friend encounters her ex and his new lover, and appears so anxious that everyone present notices her negative emotions, to not remark on her nervousness is an act of kindness, but her privacy with respect to her emotions is lost once everyone has noticed her nervousness. Of course, you could make her lose even more privacy by talking to others about this event, but merely refraining from talking about her anxiety to her does not make her regain the privacy she lost with respect to you, her ex, and her ex's lover.

What is happening in those situations is very well described by Elizabeth Strout in her novel *My Name Is Lucy Barton*:

> I suspect I said nothing because I was doing what I have done most of my life, which is to cover for the mistakes of others when they don't know they have embarrassed themselves. I do this, I think, because it could be me a great deal of the time. I know faintly, even now, that I have embarrassed myself. [. . .] But still—I do it for others, even as I sense that others do it for me.[14]

Distinguishing between self-presentation and privacy is particularly important to develop a good understanding of the social and moral pitfalls of the online world.

II. Self-Presentation Online

There is broad agreement about the benefits of having some degree of control over one's self-presentation. First, that kind of control allows us to cultivate different kinds of relationships.[15] Second, having harmonious social lives would

---

13. Carissa Véliz, 'On Privacy' (dissertation, Faculty of Philosophy, University of Oxford, 2017).

14. See Elizabeth Strout, *My Name Is Lucy Barton* (New York: Penguin, 2016), pp. 111–12. In this case, Lucy is talking about people who do not know they have embarrassed themselves, but that does not make a difference for our purposes.

15. Rachels, 'Why Privacy Is Important'.

be impossible if we could know everything about everyone at all times, and if we acted in accordance with how we feel at every moment.[16] Some degree of concealment, reticence, and nonacknowledgement is necessary to avoid unnecessary conflict in the public sphere.[17] Such limits protect both the individual, from undue judgement from other people, and the public sphere, which ends up being much less toxic if it only gets exposed to the more polished aspects of individuals, as opposed to the unadulterated versions.

It is also clear that there can be such a thing as too much control over self-presentation. No one who is not a doctor, for instance, should be able to self-present as a doctor, among other reasons, because it could be dangerous to prospective patients. If self-presentation comes too much under the complete control of individuals, people could concoct fantastical identities, potentially leading to 'manipulation, dishonesty', and a 'lack of authenticity'.[18]

One of the elements that Cocking and van den Hoven identify as leading to evil behavior online is the ability for people to self-present on their own terms. In the offline world, they note, our presentation of the self is often rich with undertones and aspects of expression that are not fully under our control. For instance, we may want to present a calm version of ourselves, but our biting our nails might betray our feelings of anxiety. Such richness of experience in face-to-face interactions allow us to 'form impressions' that 'guide our interactions' with other people.[19] Online, they argue, one can construct a whole identity largely detached from the influence of others 'and the realities of non-virtual worlds that might disrupt the identity constructed on one's own terms'.[20] Hence the famous meme about anonymity online, 'On the internet, nobody knows you're a dog', first published in the *New Yorker* by Peter Steiner in 1993.

If we were to equate self-presentation with privacy, that would lead us to conclude that one problem with social media is that people have too much privacy online, since they have too much control over their self-presentation. Andrei Marmor has recently taken that stance.[21] On that account, the solution is to further erode privacy online, requiring even more data from people. In opposition to this view, I will argue that the Internet would be a better place if people had, on the one hand, more privacy and, on the other, less control over their self-presentation.

---

16. Cocking and van den Hoven, *Evil Online*, pp. 65–66.
17. Thomas Nagel, 'Concealment and Exposure', *Philosophy and Public Affairs*, 27, no. 1 (1998), 3–30.
18. Marmor, 'What Is the Right', p. 7.
19. Cocking and van den Hoven, *Evil Online*, p. 62.
20. Cocking and van den Hoven, pp. 74–75.
21. Andrei Marmor, 'Privacy in Social Media', in *Oxford Handbook of Digital Ethics*, edited by Carissa Véliz (Oxford: Oxford University Press, forthcoming).

Before I make that argument, it is worth assessing to what extent people have more control over their self-presentation online than in the offline world, and to what extent that leads to undesirable consequences. As Cocking and van den Hoven admit, there are certain reality checks that can be provided online regarding the people we interact with, and often the online and offline worlds provide reality checks on one another.[22]

There are at least three reasons for why people might not be able to self-present completely on their own terms online. First, it seems that most people with profiles online connect to their offline relationships online, such that, if I were to purport to be a physician online, people who know me offline could call me on it. Second, people who have online profiles are incredibly exposed to input from others. In many ways, we are more exposed to each other online than offline. Offline we are usually exposed to a relatively small community, with many people either caring about us or caring about their own standing in the community—both of those concerns acting as a deterrent for evil behavior. Online we are potentially exposed to millions of strangers the world over who probably have little concern about us and do not think that their behavior will affect their standing in their communities. If people online were not so exposed to others, 'doxxing'—searching and publishing private information of someone online—would not have a name or be a problem. Third, to maintain a positive image online, one has to exercise self-control, much like in the offline world, and it is common to have slips. Involuntary facial expressions can be compared to involuntary signals online: reading or responding to a message too quickly might signal a lack of self-restraint, posting at all hours of the night might betray anxiety or insomnia, and posting things you come to regret might give away too much of how you think and feel at one particular moment. In some ways, it is easier to post something stupid online than to say something stupid offline: you can quickly type something and click 'send' without the immediate feedback that can act as a deterrence in face-to-face interactions, when we read each other's reactions to what we are saying (i.e. when you see people around you looking horrified when you speak, you know it is time to shut up).

Cocking and van den Hoven argue that we lose some of the richness and pluralism of the offline self when online. Their observation could be understood as meaning that we get to know people better offline than online, but it is not always true that self-presentation offline allows us to get a better (i.e., more complete) impression of people. Many times, one gets to know people's darkest sides online. After working with one's colleagues for years, and experiencing them as generally kind and rational people, it can be shocking to see how they behave

---

22. Cocking and van den Hoven, *Evil Online*, pp. 77–78.

online. People who seem perfectly composed offline can show aggressive and even bullying behavior online that one would have never thought was possible.

All in all, it does not seem so easy to construct a perfect identity online on one's own terms. But, as Cocking and van den Hoven rightly qualify their claim a couple of times, such a possibility can *seem* achievable, even if such a feeling is all too often illusory.[23] If you build your online identity on lies, and happen to gain notoriety while doing it, chances are it will all come crumbling down sooner or later. You can have the perfect identity online until someone interferes with it, and then it can be incredibly difficult to regain your reputation—what you are shamed for can appear in the first page of an online search for all to see for a longer time than might be reasonable.

Another element of self-presentation online that might be reason for concern is the possibility that people might be anonymous online and use that anonymity for the purposes of wrongdoing. First, anonymity online is more often than not illusory: if someone wants to unveil someone else's identity, they will. The documentary *Don't F**ck with Cats* tells the story of an anonymous user who uploads a video of him killing two kittens and gets tracked down by online users. Furthermore, it is not certain that anonymity is significantly contributing to negative trends online. As mentioned before, perfectly civil academics in the offline world seem willing to act in very questionable ways on Facebook and Twitter using their real names. Further evidence can be found in a study that looked at more than 500,000 comments from around 1600 online petitions on a German platform and found that nonanonymous individuals were more aggressive than anonymous ones.[24] We can all think of notorious politicians who behave abominably online despite not being anonymous.

What I find most remarkable about how the Internet has changed self-presentation is the expectation to share more than would have been normal in a pre-Internet world. For those of us who grew up offline: could you imagine taking photographs to school of what you ate the day before to show it to your friends? Probably not. Social media has blurred the distinction between front- and backstage in many ways that are beyond the scope of this paper. But one of those ways is that we are now expected to perform on stage much more of the time. We not only work an eight-hour shift, like we used to, but now we are expected to respond to email when we get home. Your boss might ask you to promote material with your social media account. For teenagers, this pressure can be even worse. Home is no longer where social interaction ends. If they want to be popular at school, they not only have to look good during school hours but

---

23. Cocking and van den Hoven, pp. 60 and 75.

24. Katja Rost, Lea Stahel, and Bruno S. Frey, 'Digital Social Norm Enforcement: Online Firestorms in Social Media', *PLoS One*, 11, no. 6 (2016), doi: 10.1371/journal.pone.0155923.

out of school they have to show everyone how great their life is. They have to be available to answer the messages in their friends' group chat. Teenagers worry about posting pictures with friends every weekend, lest they might be thought to have no friends or no social lives. Social media pushes us to be always on display.

III. Cultivating a Culture of Privacy and Rethinking Self-Presentation Online

Cocking and van den Hoven note that '[t]he online revolution has removed, minimized, or altered much of the influence of others, and of many of the conventions, laws, and settings of our traditional worlds'.[25] Etiquette conventions about how much and what to share in public are some of the norms that have changed the most in the digital age.

People are encouraged to overshare online and engage every minute of every day because it is profitable for social media companies. The more time online, the more ads we see, the more clicks we make, the more data gets collected about us, the more ads can get sold. Part of what we need is better regulation of the data economy and, in particular, of the advertisement industry.[26] But that challenge is too broad to tackle here. Instead, I focus on cultural changes.

It might be tempting to think that if too much control over self-presentation online is a problem, because people engage in deception and other kinds of wrongdoing, then the way to solve that problem is to diminish people's privacy. In China, for instance, people registering with a new mobile phone service are obligated to provide both an ID and a face scan. We could do the same for social media users. This kind of approach is mistaken. Such measures would expose netizens even more to possible abuse and further violations of their right to privacy.

What has brought about many of the negative trends online is a lack of privacy and an excess of engagement and disinhibition—not too much privacy. We need to change the current culture of exposure online. Encouraging reticence online is a good place to start. Just like we teach our children not to talk about just anything with just anyone, there is no reason to post every thought and feeling—particularly ones that can be harmful to others, or ones that could make one particularly vulnerable to others.

---

25. Cocking and van den Hoven, Evil Online, p. 72.
26. Carissa Véliz, *Privacy Is Power*, Bantam Press, 2020.

A culture of exposure shoves people into inauthenticity. By being required by their peers to self-present all day, netizens become images or brands of themselves. People are always imperfect. If we demand perfection from them, we are inadvertently turning them into con artists. And the responsibility is not only on the person who tries to live up to that unrealistic standard of a perfect person who is broadcasting their life all day long online. Part of the responsibility for that distortion of truth lies on social media platforms, and on the users who follow such people, both to admire them while the legend lives on and to condemn them when the perfect image inevitably cracks.

When a new technology gets popularized, it often takes some time for people to adjust to it and to create adequate social norms around it. I suspect this process is still in its infancy with respect to our digital lives.

When we show a film about Superman to children, we immediately explain to them that films are fiction—real people cannot fly. Otherwise we risk them thinking they might be able to fly. In the same way, part of the social mistake in judging 'influencers' as authentic people is to not appreciate that they are nothing but advertisements. Accusing an influencer of being inauthentic is like accusing an actor of pretending to be another person. That is exactly what we are paying them to do (if not with money, with our attention). The idea of a fake influencer is an oxymoron.

Thomas Nagel points out that certain practices that are somewhat generous with the truth are not deceptive when the convention is known by all. What counts as a deception, therefore, partly depends on our audience, on whether they are willing to take what we say and do at face value: 'A visitor to a society whose conventions he does not understand may be deceived if he takes people's performance at face value—the friendliness of the Americans, the self-abnegation of the Japanese, the equanimity of the English'.[27] What I am arguing is that we need to change our social conventions on many platforms online. Too many of us too much of the time seem to be acting like clueless tourists online.

By not taking at face value what people post online—by not judging influencers as authentic people but as advertisements or brands—we take away their control to self-present on their own terms. That power is taken away because we no longer take their posts to be a self-presentation at all. Especially in the case of influencers, we ought to understand their performance much as an actor's performance. Paradoxically, that inattention to the person as a person would take some of the pressure away from flesh-and-blood people to try to pretend what they are not.

---

27. Nagel, 'Concealment and Exposure', p. 11.

Of course, what I am proposing would not work well for every platform and type of profile online. Academics on academic social media are an exception, for instance. In that case, professional reality checks already ensure that people cannot self-present on their own terms—people cannot get away with claiming a publication that is not theirs, for instance. The case of politicians on official accounts on Twitter is trickier and too complex to address in this paper.

There is also the concern that treating too much content online as fiction might lead to a disinterest in truth. One possibility to try to simplify the online landscape, and for people to more easily distinguish what ought to be taken at face value from what ought to be taken as advertisement or fiction, is to have different platforms for different purposes. Part of why the online world can be so confusing is because very different kinds of content can be found on the same platform. Just like we have a platform for academic philosophers, we could have a platform only for politicians, and a platform for influencers and similar performers.[28] Alternatively, we could tag branded content and influencers as such.

Of course, not all problems online would go away if people had more privacy and less control over their self-presentation. But giving people more privacy and less control over their self-presentation would likely help diminish online harassment because it would protect potential victims. It would also minimize unrealistic expectations about people. Elsewhere I have argued that using stable pseudonyms in much of our online life would be a good idea.[29] Pseudonyms provide privacy but also take away some control over self-presentation, as pseudonyms are not tied to our offline identities—they are taken to be fictional characters. Pseudonyms can also be a good tool to regulate without censoring speech, as they allow for nuanced penalties (such as losing one's pseudonym).

IV. Conclusion

In this paper I have argued against views that equate privacy with control over self-presentation. I have further argued that what is most notable about self-presentation online is the pressure to be on display at all times and places. As antidotes to some of the negative trends we can see on social media, I suggest cultivating a culture of privacy by discouraging self-exposure, and rethinking

---

28. This suggestion encounters the following problem: platforms tend to fund themselves through advertising, which in turn suggests that we either need to find alternative funding schemes for platforms online or we need to heavily legislate the rules of advertisement online to cause less confusion about what kind of content we are being exposed to.

29. Carissa Véliz, 'Online Masquerade: Redesigning the Internet for Free Speech through the Use of Pseudonyms', *Journal of Applied Philosophy*, 36, no. 4 (2019), pp. 643–58.

how we understand self-presentation online. I argue that, in some cases, such as that of influencers, we should take their performances to be only that—performances, like the performances of actors. By not interpreting all online personae as self-presentations, we take away some of the power for people to self-present on their own terms. Suggestions to decrease people's control over self-presentation include having different platforms for different purposes (separating the pursuit of truth, such as in academic platforms, from other kinds of pursuits), tagging fictional identities like that of influencers as such, and using pseudonyms in at least some of our online interactions. Many of the worst trends online can be partly attributed to the losses of privacy we have undergone online. The last thing we need is to have even less privacy. On the contrary, rejecting our current culture of exposure can be the first step to regaining much of what we have lost by going online.

ॐ JPE ॐ

Moral Fog and the Appreciation of Value

DEAN COCKING
Delft Design for Values Institute

JEROEN VAN DEN HOVEN
Delft University of Technology

Keywords: value appreciation, moral fog, 'unselfing', social dependence, moral education, intimacy.

By opening our eyes we do not necessarily see what confronts us. We are anxiety-ridden animals. Our minds are continually active, fabricating an anxious, usually self-preoccupied, often falsifying *veil* which partially conceals the world. Our states of consciousness differ in quality. [. . .] And if quality matters, then anything which alters consciousness in the direction of unselfishness, objectivity and realism is to be connected with virtue.

—Iris Murdoch, 'The Sovereignty of Good Over Other Concepts'

Who you gonna believe, me or your own eyes?

—Chico Marx, *Duck Soup*

Introduction

We are delighted to have this wonderful opportunity to develop our thinking about the problem of 'moral fog' and of the flourishing of evil online. We owe special thanks to Roger Crisp for his significant help in developing our thoughts

Contact: Dean Cocking <dean.cocking@bigpond.com>
     https://orcid.org/0000-0002-2590-4925
     Jeroen van den Hoven <M.J.vandenHoven@tudelft.nl>
     https://orcid.org/0000-0003-2376-3185

https://doi.org/10.3998/jpe.1182

over the past two years and for his terrific work as editor for this special issue.[1] We are also very grateful to Dale Dorsey, Philip Kitcher, and Carissa Véliz for their thoughtful and varied commentaries and the many helpful suggestions and directions they have given us.

In response, we have developed our account of the moral fog to show how it describes foundational problems for human capacities to appreciate value. We provide a diagnosis of the primary sources of the problem, and we describe how increasingly living online has fueled these wellsprings in spectacularly additional and distinctive ways. The enabling (or otherwise) of our capacities for value appreciation is fundamental to our prospects for moral progress. Thus, a focus on value appreciation and the problem of moral fog, we argue, provides foundational (and much needed) criteria and guidelines for the normative assessment and regulation of our lives, especially now as we increasingly live online and the fog around valuing thickens.

Our discussion proceeds in two sections. In section 1 we describe the primary sources of moral fog and how these have been built upon and expanded by increasingly living online. In section 2 we describe the social dependence of valuing and how some important morally educative social practices helping us out of our fog have also been lost and corrupted online.

Unselfing in the Age of the Selfie

The Fog for Appreciating Value

How does a schoolyard friend become an online bully? How do shy kids become super-spreaders of hate speech? How can we be more connected than ever yet loneliness has become a major health issue? How did the online revolution go from a great leap forward for democracy to a great leap backward? How did the authority of reason and science become social conspiracy, part of some matrix of illusion? Moral progress relies on the idea that our capacities for making good judgments are getting better. As we increasingly live online, however, we have reason to worry they are getting worse.

Good judgment is dependent upon our more basic and broader capacities for value appreciation. Value appreciation, along with our abilities for governance by it, lie at the core of our nature as moral beings.[2] Our capacities to appreciate

---

1. Thanks also to Tom Douglas for his excellent editorial suggestions.

2. As R. Jay Wallace puts it, 'What is valuable about persons is precisely their capacity to appreciate and respond to the good". See, R. Jay Wallace, ed., *The Practice of Value (The Berkeley Tanner Lectures)* (Oxford: Oxford University Press, 2003), p. 4. We make use of this excellent collection throughout our discussion and are greatly indebted to it.

and respond to value, however, are limited and vulnerable in many ways. We are all, much of the time (more or less) in something of a moral fog, our appreciation of value clouded, as Iris Murdoch describes, by 'falsifying veils'.[3] Our increasingly living online (however) has poured rocket fuel onto the problem.

Many are worried about the kind of rhetorical questions above and the fate of the moral life as we increasingly live online. Political scientists and observers, for example, worry about the fate of democracy as corporate and political organizations collect unprecedented data about what makes us tick, making us more vulnerable to manipulation and misinformation than ever. As Philip Kitcher describes, the approximation to something like a 'reasonably informed citizen' upon which the success of representative democracy depends now seems especially at risk.[4] Further, many social scientists and commentators are worried about the fate of our personal lives and of the broader relational fabric of society. For instance, while we have more 'social connection' in our new online worlds than previously imaginable, we are seemingly lonelier than ever.[5] Similarly, many worry about young people growing up online and how this is shaping their understanding of self and others. One problem, for example, is that life online is making them (even) more insecure, overly focused on their online likes, visits, and self-promotion.[6]

Iris Murdoch highlights one central kind of problem for our capacities for value appreciation. She describes how our condition as self-conscious beings brings with it a self-preoccupation that is anxiety-ridden and selfish and how both undermine our capacities to appreciate value.[7] Improving our capacities

---

3. Christine Korsgaard claims the source of our capacity for valuing lies in our capacity for normative or evaluative self-conception and describes how this can make us vulnerable to a whole set of external influences that distort our values. See Christine Korsgaard, 'Eternal Values, Evolving Values', in reply to Ian Morris's *Foragers, Farmers and Fossil Fuel* (Princeton, NJ: Princeton University Press, 2015), pp 184–201. She says, for instance, 'Our sense of self-worth makes us vulnerable to all kinds of influences, and those influences work by distorting our values' (p. 193). Korsgaard associates these distortions with 'ideologies'. We suggest they are no less associated with our sociotechnical milieu.

4. Philip Kitcher, 'Losing Your Way in the Fog: Reflections on *Evil Online*', p. 19.

5. As Sherry Turkle describes, we are 'maximally connected' but 'alone together'. See Sherry Turkle, *Alone Together: Why We Expect More from Technology and Less from Each Other* (New York: Basic Books, 2011). Loneliness has now been widely recognized as a major health issue. In 2018, for instance, the United Kingdom introduced what is loosely known as a 'ministry for loneliness' to make the reduction of loneliness an ongoing parliamentary concern.

6. See, e.g., the large research project concerning how social media influences education and psychological development, Howard Gardner and Katie Davis, *The App Generation: How Today's Youth Navigate Identity, Intimacy and Imagination in a Digital World* (New Haven, CT: Yale University Press, 2013), pp. 75–86.

7. Murdoch seems to run together selfishness with the anxiety-ridden self, but much anxiety-ridden self-preoccupation does not seem well captured by selfishness, such as widespread insecurities about looking ugly or stupid. The more general problem Murdoch has in mind that

for value appreciation, then, requires that we 'unself' from this anxiety-ridden selfishness of our self-consciousness.[8] Social media, however, enhances this malady of the modern liberal individual where thinking of oneself dominates and frames how one thinks of others and the world around oneself.

Like us, Murdoch points to a problem of moral fog as a fundamental obstacle for moral understanding, education, and progress. Our 'preoccupied self-concern' presents a widely shared important source of the problem since it comes with our condition as self-conscious beings. In addition to various problems that *we* bring to the table are the falsifying influences *others* bring.[9] Chico Marx draws our attention to this second, central kind of vulnerability involved in our capacities for value appreciation—namely, their dependence upon the help, or otherwise, we get from others. Our understanding, our capacities for understanding, are unavoidably and deeply dependent upon others and the world around us. This social dependence of value appreciation very much includes our abilities to see and unself from falsifying aspects of ourselves, such as our self-conscious anxieties and selfishness. Thus, our two vulnerabilities often come together.

For better or worse, we see ourselves and understand much of what we see through the lead of others and our settings. Our intimate relations are especially crucial enablers (or otherwise) of self-understanding, including in regard to falsifying aspects of self. This dependence and vulnerability are the conditions 'gaslighting' trades on, why it can work so well, and what Marx turns into a reductio. Moreover, our need for help is not confined to the extremes of our 'early' years (along with our 'later' ones). We continue to be unavoidably dependent upon others and our settings for knowledge, understanding, value appreciation, and virtue, such as when we enter new areas with which we are relatively unfamiliar.[10]

---

would include a broader suite of self-regarding attitudes is the relentless self-concern of self-consciousness. As we say above, we think the more fundamental features sourcing moral fog are our subjectivity and contingency. Iris Murdoch, 'The Sovereignty of Good Over Other Concepts', *The Virtues: Contemporary Essays on Moral Character*, ed. Robert B. Kruschwitz and Robert C. Roberts (Belmont, CA: Wadsworth Publishing Company, 1987), pp. 84–98.

8. Many and varied views about values, and of the quality of consciousness required to appreciate them, describe the need for some kind of 'unselfing'. For example, Kant's metaphysic of the moral comprehensively annexed the empirical self and Buddhists describe transcendence to value appreciation in terms of the dissolving of 'self'.

9. Robert Frank refers to behavioural externalities that can be both positive and negative. On the negative, for instance, he says, 'By analogy to the economist's language for describing the harm caused by environmental pollution, I refer to the effects of the latter environments as negative behavioural externalities'. Robert H. Frank, *Under the Influence: Putting Peer Pressure to Work* (Princeton, NJ: Princeton University Press, 2020), pp. 191–92, Kindle ed.

10. See, e.g., chapter 4 of *Evil Online* where we describe our learning vulnerabilities and how they help explain the behaviour of subjects in many of our famous social science experiments, including, for instance, Solomon Asch's original 'obedience' experiments, Stanley Milgram's

There is now widespread attention across mainstream media to various disturbing cases and trends flourishing online, and many recognize the need for much greater regulation. Likewise, there is a rapidly increasing movement of philosophical and ethical analysis of life online. Current discussions, however, remain in need of a foundational normative approach to guide analyses of life online and to guide how we should think about and pursue greater regulation. Better understanding our capacities for value appreciation, in particular their limits and distortions and what helps and hinders them, is fundamental to better understanding the human pursuit of virtue and a worthwhile life. As such, a focus on our capacities for value appreciation provides a foundational guide for thinking about moral education and about the ethical design and regulation of our lives in the digital age. Everyone agrees that online platforms need to be designed in more value-sensitive ways, and value-sensitive design approaches have largely focused on giving values, such as respect or empathy, far more presence online. However, as Murdoch and Marx describe, we often fail to see what is right in front of us. Thus, even if our values have some presence, falsifying influences within us, and from others and our surrounds, commonly undermine our capacities to appreciate and respond to value.

The moral fog describes this general problem for our valuing, how our appreciation of value is limited, distorted, or out of focus altogether. This can be both because values have little presence in our environment to direct our focus and help guide us and because even when our values do have presence, we nevertheless (commonly) fail to appreciate them. We take decades to mature and are utterly reliant upon relatively functional moral (and mortal) education to do so. Moreover, absent moral maintenance (guides and censures) from the personal and sociopolitical worlds within which we find ourselves, we cannot expect too much clearing of the fog from our more mature, even morally well-educated, approximations to personhood. Moral fog remains because two fundamental features of our nature generate limits, distortions, and a lack of focus that produce it: our subjectivity and contingency. The problem is significant because of the significance of the limitations and distortions our subjectivity presents for value appreciation and the fleeting, fragile experiences our contingency allows for it.

Murdoch points the finger at our condition of self-consciousness, and the anxiety-ridden self-preoccupation it produces, as the source of the falsifying

---

'electro-shock' experiments, and Philip Zimbardo's 'Stanford Prison' experiment. As we also describe below, Aristotle highlights a strong ongoing dependence of our virtue on others and our sociopolitical surrounds—hence, for instance, the move to politics at the end of the *Nicomachean Ethics*; see, *N.E.*, X.9. Aristotle, *Nichomachean Ethics*, trans. W. D. Ross (Oxford: Oxford University Press, 1980).

veils for our capacities to appreciate value. We claim our conditions of subjective perspective and focus and of contingent possibilities for experience, reflection, and valuing as the fundamental wellsprings of moral fog. The fog of our anxiety-ridden self-preoccupation does not result *just* from our condition as self-conscious beings but also (or more so) from the limitations and distortions of our subjectivity and contingent possibilities for value appreciation. These limits and distortions present fundamental vulnerabilities undermining our pursuit of reality and value about which (in broad terms at least) we are very conscious. As a result, our self-awareness is also very much focused on these vulnerabilities and generates similarly fundamental anxieties, insecurities, and self-obsessions.

So how and why might things be getting worse as we live online? Let us begin with the main approach taken by those who think things are not getting worse or, if they are, that online communication is not the culprit.

'It's Just a Tool'

In an interview from 1999 (now widely circulated on social media) with Jeremy Paxman of the BBC, David Bowie talked about the Internet and the revolutionary forum for individual rebellion, expression, and creativity it seemed to promise. One especially apt exchange went like this:

Paxman: "You don't think some of the claims being made for it [the Internet] are hugely exaggerated? When the telephone was invented people made amazing claims [about how it would change the world]."

Bowie: "I know the president at the time was outrageous; he said he foresaw the day when every town in America would have a telephone [. . .] how dare he [. . .] absolute bullshit (laughs). No, you see I don't agree. I don't think we've seen even the tip of the iceberg. [. . .] I think the potential [. . .] both good and bad [. . .] is unimaginable. [. . .] I think we're actually on the cusp of something both exhilarating and terrifying."

Paxman: "It's just a tool though isn't it?"

Bowie: "No it's not [. . .] no. It's an alien life form (laughs)".[11]

---

11. 'David Bowie speaks to Jeremy Paxman on BBC Newsnight (1999)', YouTube, https://www.bing.com/videos/search?q=davif+bowie+interview+1999+bbc&docid=608055566860224755&mid=1DB99748C5E6A18040971DB99748C5E6A1804097&view=detail&FORM=VIRE [accessed 28 August 2020].

There is a long and continuing history of appealing to the description 'it's *just* a tool' to account for the Internet and our use of it, as Moira Weigel illustrates (along with Mark Zuckerberg's relentless use of the description) in 'Silicon Valley's Sixty Year Love Affair with the Word "Tool" '.[12] Dale Dorsey takes the baton for this approach in this volume, claiming that the distinguishing feature of the Internet from pre-Internet life is (simply) that the Internet is a spectacular tool for effective communication. As a result, while it has caused evil to be communicated more effectively, it has likewise promoted the good more effectively. The medium itself, however, on this view, is neither good nor bad; it is just a great communication tool.[13]

First, however, (generally speaking) tools are not '*just* tools'. If something generates (or risks) notable normative effects (not just, e.g., by accident), then we cannot adequately describe that something without mention of them. Asbestos is an excellent building material in various ways, affording all sorts of terrific advances, including insulation, strength, flexibility, and durability. Unfortunately, it can also break down, release fibers into the atmosphere, and kill you. Accordingly, if you wanted to know about asbestos, these things would be important to know. If, for example, one had to sit a test to show an adequate knowledge of asbestos, one would not pass that test by declaring, 'It's *just* a building material'. Likewise, the goose that laid the golden egg was not just a goose, nor the egg just an egg. 'It's *just* a tool' (like 'it's *just* my work' or 'it's *just* business' in other contexts) is a reductive (mis)description that is invariably used to turn our focus away from appreciating the *dis*value attached to the Internet.

Moreover, even where there are significant goods to be achieved by 'proper' use of X, we err on the side of caution where misuse of X may also cause significantly bad effects. Hence, despite the revolutionary advances it offered as a building material, we ban or very strictly regulate the use of asbestos. We certainly do not allow, for example, children and young people to use it. Thus, even if we focus on the 'it *just* depends upon how you use it' part of the description (rather than the 'it's *just* a tool' part), the problem of setting aside the (important) normative realities attached to using the thing remains. Indeed, it is not only children, young people, and others lacking some competence that need help

---

12. Moira Weigel, 'Silicon Valley's Sixty Year Love Affair with the Word "Tool" ', *New Yorker*, 12 April 2018. For a collection of recent defenders of the theme that 'tech is a just a tool', see Pew Research Center, 'Tech Is (Just) a Tool', https://www.pewresearch.org/internet/2020/06/30/tech-is-just-a-tool accessed 4 January 2021).

13. Dale Dorsey, 'Moral Intensifiers and the Efficiency of Communication', p. 6.

online. Living in virtual worlds compounds problems of moral fog for otherwise normal, well-adjusted, and fortunate (enough) adults.[14]

The distinguishing mark of Internet communication compared to that before, says Dale Dorsey, is simply *the efficiency of communication* online.[15] Dorsey's main theme against our claims concerning the proliferation in degree and kind of evils online is to query or deny that they 'are representative of our lives online or, indeed, have anything to do with the existence of the Internet per se'.[16] He suggests, instead, that the efficiency of Internet communication and the resultant amplification of views explains any increase in evils online and explains away our claims of new *kinds* of evils flourishing online. He makes his case in reply to a few of our examples, such as a case of rape filmed and spread online and the erosion of the plural worlds and related values of the public and private realms online.[17] In the rape case, however, it seems clear that it would not have been 'half the fun' had it not been filmed, commented upon, and shared online. Moreover, while appalling acts of such sorts have, of course, long occurred, this case is just one of many we give that highlights the additional traction provided by the online context, such as, for example, the online *trend* of 'happy slapping' where harm is done *for* the attention it will get when uploaded and maximally shared.[18]

---

14. In her essay 'Liberal Man', Susan Mendus describes an important form of fog that comes with our increasing engagement with technology—that we increasingly think of *ourselves* as tools: 'In the pursuit of technological omnipotence man becomes more like a tool himself. His value is no longer an intrinsic value, defined by reference of his neediness, but an instrumental value, defined in terms of the power he can exert over other things" (p. 51). See Susan Mendus, 'Liberal Man', in *Philosophy and Politics*, ed. G.M.K. Hunt (London: Royal Institute of Philosophy, 1990), pp. 45–59.

15. See, p. 6. Dorsey says he agrees that the efficiency of the medium spreads evil more efficiently; however, he suggests, it also spreads much good more efficiently. Hence, he thinks, the efficiency does not tend toward evildoing especially. The efficiency of the medium is 'janus-faced' he says. (p. 12) We allow that many of the features of the medium are 'janus-faced', giving traction to both evil and good online (*Evil Online*, p. 38). Thus, we agree, like many technologies, significant effects, both good and bad, often result from the same considerations. If the bads, however, are very notable, then we have serious cause for concern about any given consideration, even if it also produces some important goods. This is precisely Kitcher's point (against us): What good does it achieve if we get all the knowledge of Wiki but the same explosion in information and unregulated access to all manner of views is also accelerating the demise of democracy and of the planet? Our main point, of course, is that the issue is not just about one consideration, such as efficiency broadly construed. Instead, the problems giving evil online special traction are something of a 'perfect storm' of factors, which together really do produce evils not only of greater magnitude but of different kinds.

16. Dorsey, 'Moral Intensifiers', p. 7.

17. Dorsey, pp. 7–8.

18. In 'Mass Murder of, and for, the Internet' Kevin Roose describes how the attacks on two mosques in Christchurch, New Zealand, that killed fifty-one people were fueled by the pursuit of attention on the Internet. See Roose, 'Mass Murder of, and for, the Internet', *New York Times*, 15 May 2019, https://www.nytimes.com/2019/03/15/technology/facebook-youtube-christ-church-shooting.html.

In reply to our worries about the demolition of the plural worlds of public and private life, Dorsey gives the example of young girls posting advertisements in magazines in the pre-Internet world to trade personal information for personal connection—a long-standing trade-off by teenagers, he notes. Thus, even if we are right and the revolution of living our social lives online has undertaken a demolition job on public/private contrasts, this remains only a difference in degree. However, as we live online and the demolition of public/private contrasts grows in magnitude in our lives, then, as we argued in *Evil Online*,[19] we lose and distort many important values in additional and distinctive ways.

Amplification often produces significant changes and distortions that transform the content that results and so the *kind* of thing (such as the kind of communication tool) that is produced. Jimi Hendrix provided many spectacular practical demonstrations of how amplification produces distortion to transform content and the kind of communication provided by electric guitar. Joseph Raz gives us a compelling general theoretical explanation of how matters of degree can change the kind of things that result. As Raz explains, something can (more or less) be a kind of a thing, a bad example of that thing, or no example at all, depending upon the degrees to which it instantiates the ideal standards defining that kind of thing. Relaxation, for example, might be an important ideal standard for defining what counts as a good holiday. Thus, as one's 'holiday' becomes less relaxing it becomes (in this respect) less of a holiday. If it becomes extremely stressful it may be no holiday at all. Indeed, it may become something from which one very much needs a holiday.[20]

The massive amplification of views and issues resulting from the revolutionary 'efficiency' of communication Dorsey describes has generated a very different landscape of social discourse. It has resulted, for example, in a sea of misinformation, giving special traction to widespread confusion and rejection of truth, both scientific and moral, of the most important kinds, such as the rejection of science about climate change and the rapid destruction of the planet. The amplification has also brought about the perverse celebration of many moral horrors and tragedies by enabling a community to normalize them and promote them as cool lifestyles or forms of entertainment, thereby obscuring focus on their (otherwise loud and clear) disvalue. A striking recent example is given by Forrest Stuart in *Ballad of the Bullet: Gangs, Drill Music, and the Power of Online*

---

19. Dean Cocking and Jeroen van den Hoven, *Evil Online* (New York: Wiley, 2018).

20. Raz's gives the example of a 'holiday' to provide the explanation, and we run with it here. See Wallace, *The Practice of Value*, p. 32, note 18. In our example of the 'Hendrix effect', the kind of musical communication provided by electric guitar was expanded and transformed by (his use of) the distorting effects of amplification.

Infamy.[21] In this case, gang violence and ghetto life are celebrated and sold to the huge market for 'public voyeurism' related to such horrors and tragedies that has been enabled online. ('Drill music' refers to the music the gangs use during their gun violence.[22])

Doubling Down on 'Selfing'

The contemporary age of the 'selfie' is spectacular icing on the cake of our recent centuries of self.[23] We now, for example, talk about ourselves far more as we live online. Figures vary, but all agree the increase is significant (some sources say the increase is around twice as much, others say it is around fifty percent).[24] It is not, however, just that as *individuals* we talk more about ourselves or that we are engaged in more presentations of self. The preoccupation with self is crucially enabled by the fact that it is a *community* of people talking about one another's talk about themselves. In fact, it is a global community normalizing discourse that is overly engaged in reflecting back to one another everyone's talk about themselves. As Joey Borelli (@joeybtoonz) joked, "Narcissism used to be a bad thing!?"[25] As a global community, we are driving ourselves and one another back into ourselves and doubling down on 'selfing'.

Actor Jack Nicholson observed that everybody has a problem with celebrity. In *Evil Online*, we also quote some interesting observations from actor/

---

21. Forrest Stuart, *Ballad of the Bullet: Gangs, Drill Music and the Power of Online Infamy* (Princeton, NJ: Princeton University Press, 2020).

22. Dorsey queries our suggestion that various extreme evils, such as the proliferation of terrorism or proanorexia sites, are not just minor dark alleys of the internet (p. 9). He notes, using some figures we cite of the staggering explosion of overall Internet traffic, that these evils may only represent a minor part of overall Internet traffic. Fair enough. Nevertheless, of course, it is true and far more importantly so, that evils such as terrorism, harmful pseudo-science, child porn, and so on have exploded with the advent of the Internet. Moreover, as we describe in the book, there are many extreme evils that have been especially facilitated by the Internet. None need in themselves, of course, count for much as a proportion of overall Internet traffic. But the ongoing relentless explosion of degrees and kinds of such extreme moral horrors (filling newspapers, books, investigative stories every other day) is remarkable and alarming. In any case, the prevalence across social life of the doubling down on selfing we highlight is certainly a notable part of the core business of Internet life.

23. The BBC documentary series *The Century of the Self* provides many insights about the rise of our self-preoccupation over the past 100 years. See *The Century of the Self*, BBC and RDF Television, 2002.

24. See, for example, Courtney Seiter, 'The Psychology of Social Media: Why We Like, Comment, and Share Online', Buffer, 10 August 2016, https://buffer.com/resources/psychology-of-social-media/.

25. See joeybtoonz, 'Narcissists and #SOCIALMEDIA', YouTube, https://www.youtube.com/c/joeybtoonz [accessed 20 January 2021].

filmmaker Clint Eastwood on fame and how, with fame, due to everyone relating to a famous person as their famous image, it becomes impossible to observe, much less relate to, people just being themselves. The world of engagement with others becomes largely reduced to interacting with their celebrity self that is reflected back to them in the eyes and behavior of others.[26] Thus, others are unable to see and interact with the famous person and the famous person does not get to see and interact with them. For an actor, this is a problem since they are no longer presented with a variety of human expressions and behaviors from which they can learn how to act. All of us, however, increasingly preoccupied with our virtual self-presentations on social media have inherited much the same problem. Whether about our fame or not about fame at all, preoccupation with (virtual) images of ourselves overly shapes our self-expression, communication, and shared activity with one another.

The main features driving our preoccupation with self across our major social media platforms are the dominance of comparative-competitive connections fueled by likes, clicks, and views[27]; the hyper-personalization enabled by the use of artificial intelligence and 'big data' to microtarget and influence the behavior of individuals; the dominance of connections of weak ties with one another (commonly seeming to substitute for strong ones)[28]; the objectification of one another, marginalizing and denying subjectivity with reductions of one another to images and texts[29]; and the business model driven by big data about what makes us tick, manipulating and commodifying us, selling us to those wanting to influence us 24/7.[30]

The recent book *Grandstanding: The Use and Abuse of Moral Talk*[31] provides an excellent example of one notable trend in which we are doubling down on selfing online and as a result compounding our problems with foggy capacities for value appreciation. The 'grandstander' (much like the 'virtue-signaler') has

---

26. Interview with Andrew Denton, *Enough Rope*, ABC Television, Australia, 24 November 2008.

27. *Some* measures have been taken to redress the problem, such as the removal of publicly displaying how many 'likes' everyone gets on Instagram.

28. On 'strong and weak ties' and an interesting discussion of the importance of 'weak' ties, e.g., for social comparison, support, and the spread of ideas and information, see Malcolm R. Parks, 'Weak and Strong Tie Relationships', Wiley Online Library, https://onlinelibrary.wiley.com/doi/abs/10.1002/9781118540190.wbeic041 [accessed 1 March 2022].

29. See, for example, Martha Nussbaum's discussion of objectification online, 'Internet Misogyny and Objectification', in *The Offensive Internet* (Cambridge, MA: Harvard University Press, 2010).

30. These features have been widely canvassed. They are the main worries about living online presented, for instance, in the film *The Social Dilemma*, dir. Jeff Orlowski (Boulder, CO: Exposure Labs, 2020).

31. Justin Tosi and Brandon Warmke, *Grandstanding: The Use and Abuse of Moral Talk* (Oxford: Oxford University Press, 2020).

their positive self-image as the righteous espouser of certain values as their primary governing concern rather than the value they are grandstanding about. The case provides a good example of how the dominance of comparative-competitive connections that drives online preoccupation with self is commonly played out and seems especially interesting for our purposes here, since (of course) there cannot be any question about whether values are present and on the radar for the user—the grandstander is grandstanding about them. Nevertheless, by grandstanding about them, their own self-promotion becomes the governing value, in turn marginalizing appreciation of the value about which they are grandstanding.

There is obviously a lot of grandstanding going on across our social media platforms and in all sorts of ways.[32] If we look, for example, at our own field on Twitter (the community of 'academic twitter') there is a lot of 'humblebragging' going on: 'I am so proud to be invited to contribute', and so on. In fact, it is remarkable how many of us are incredibly honored to be who we are on account of some recent book, appointment, recognition, or association we are claiming to be 'honoring'. The case of grandstanding also draws our attention to another way in which amplification online distorts and changes the messages we take on. For the amplification affords not only more attention to the specific content one is ostensibly communicating. The amplification also brings far more attention to oneself. The person sending the message (or their profile) is also amplified. As a result, the messages, or kind of thing that becomes the main concern of the communication, often changes. The message of the grandstander was supposed to be, for example, that value X needs to be far more appreciated. The grandstander, however, embracing or caught up in the amplification afforded by the medium, is now focused on grandstanding. Due to a combination of features concerning the design of the medium, such as the amplification of attention to virtual images of self, and features of the milieu, such as the amplification of competitive-comparative self/other understandings, the amplification effects of the medium go well beyond amplifying the content of information or ideas in a message.[33] Indeed, for the grandstander, the content of the message about value

---

32. While Tosi and Warmke note how grandstanding has been around forever, they also recognize some ways in which the Internet has given it special traction, such as by pushing us to extremes to 'stand out in saturated waters' and how this changes the message. See, e.g., Tosi and Warmke, 'Preface', *Grandstanding*, p. xi.

33. There are many features providing traction to such problems of polarizing and extreme and intolerant views flourishing online, such as filter bubbles and echo chambers. Most significant of all, we argue, is the absence of so much of the moral terrain and language we have built upon this terrain to enable value appreciation, such as much of the rich and nuanced suite of face-to-face communications we have developed over many thousands of years to help inform and navigate our interactions with one another.

X needing to be better appreciated now takes a back seat to the preoccupation with self (with promoting virtual and virtuous images of oneself) that is also 'amplified' by the medium.

As Herbert Simon sharply observed, the only thing that is scarce when information is abundant is attention.[34] Furthermore, how much attention one gets determines the value of that attention, hence there is a massive positional arms race for attention online. Without building a presence online, increasing the number of Twitter followers, putting oneself 'out there', grandstanding, saying outrageous things, or publishing papers that will 'shit-stir',[35] one will not be visible or will be far less visible in the sea of others who are already so heavily engaged in such self-presentations and promotion. In focusing on the parameters of online attention there is a shift away from tracking, toward getting attention and away from the things that warrant attention. In this way, intrinsic motivations concerned with pursuing or promoting value are 'crowded out' by instrumental rewards such as likes, views, and followers.[36] It may even become more difficult to get valuing started. For instance, in a large survey among young people regarding the most popular career they wanted to pursue, a remarkable shift has occurred in the last decade: doctor, pilot, scientist, and musician have been replaced by 'influencer' and 'vlogger'.[37] Here the indicia of social recognition and measurable attention for activity comes first, the attention 'cart' (increasingly) comes before the value 'horse', and our transcendence to becoming valued beings or to becoming persons gets sidelined from the very start.

---

34. See, Herbert A. Simon, *Designing Organizations for an Information-Rich World* (Baltimore, MD: Johns Hopkins University Press, 1971) pp. 37–52. Simon says, '[I]n an information-rich world, the wealth of information means a dearth of something else: a scarcity of whatever it is that information consumes. What information consumes is rather obvious: it consumes the attention of its recipients. Hence a wealth of information creates a poverty of attention and a need to allocate that attention efficiently among the overabundance of information sources that might consume it' (pp. 40–41).

35. See Nicholas Agar, 'On the Moral Obligation to Stop Shit-Stirring', *Psyche*, December 2020.

36. Robert Frank, for instance, provides compelling demonstrations of how these positional arms races are socially wasteful and alienate us from what is valuable. See Robert H. Frank, *The Darwin Economy: Liberty, Competition, and the Common Good* (Princeton, NJ: Princeton University Press, 2011). See also the work of Sam Bowles for an analysis of how external rewards and pecuniary incentives for activities, where there were initially intrinsic motivations and moral reasons, undermine and crowd out the latter motives and reasons by being associated with financial consequences that are not internally related to those valued practices. Samuel Bowles, *The Moral Economy: Why Good Incentives Are No Substitute for Good Citizens* (New Haven, CT: Yale University Press, 2016).

37. See Chloe Taylor, 'Kids Now Dream of Being Professional YouTubers Rather Than Astronauts, Study Finds', CNBC, 19 July 2019, https://www.cnbc.com/2019/07/19/more-children-dream-of-being-youtubers-than-astronauts-lego-says.html.

The main game of Internet use is the pursuit of social life online. Social connections online are heavily influenced by a cluster of features that compound undesirable forms of selfing, such as 'weak ties' substituting for 'strong ties' to one another, the personalization of filter bubbles and echo chambers, the absence and obfuscation of subjectivity and of the navigational support of a suite of moral guides and forms of censure. The pursuit of social life online is now the primary way through which many pursue social life. The pursuit of social life online is also now the primary form of Internet use and so responsible for a very notable slice of the staggering amount of overall Internet traffic. Thus, the worries about the social evils involved in doubling down on selfing as we increasingly live online are of pervasive concern.[38]

In stark contrast to Dorsey, Philip Kitcher suggests we might not go far enough in characterizing the dangers of living online. He recognizes that many of the concerns we raise in discussing particular cases, pathologies, and trends are 'bigger-picture' concerns about the 'potential for huge damage to human lives and to human society' (p. 20). He says, however, we could have gone further across two fronts. First, in regard to the damage done to knowledge and understanding. We note in *Evil Online* some of the revolutionary epistemic benefits of the Internet. We also, as Kitcher wants to highlight, describe some of the great epistemic threats of the Internet, such as to the development of the 'reasonably well-informed citizen' needed for democracy to work and the flourishing of all kinds of pseudo-science. Kitcher is right to ask, however, 'What does it profit a species to gain the entire wisdom of Wikipedia, and lose both the best (or least bad?) form of government and its planet as well?' (p. 19).

Kitcher shares our concern about limits and distortions in the capacities of individuals for good judgement and also points to the dependence of the individual's virtue upon society and the (long history of) development of moral educative social practices:

> We are able on occasion to recognize the goals and aspirations of others, and to modify our own actions so that they harmonize. Yet this ability

---

38. Dorsey also takes issue (pp. 10–11) with our running together of the moral and prosocial in *Evil Online*. We can, of course, distinguish between the moral and the prosocial. Indeed, sometimes we must, such as when the immorality of an actual social world's stance on something needs to be exposed. Even here, however, the stance is immoral because it is not *really* prosocial at all, such as with all forms of prejudice. Dorsey is pointing to how the moral and social can come apart by pointing to how (more) ideal moral worlds and actual social worlds can come apart. More ideal social worlds, however, will, of course, not merely be social by conventional standards but by moral ones. We assume (moral) ideals of the 'social' when we run the moral and prosocial together, as do discussions concerning the various social psychology experiments we also wanted to include and address in our analysis of the immorality and corruption of normal people.

frequently breaks down, and we thwart the intentions of people with whom we causally interact. The moral project amplifies our responsiveness. The shortcomings of our evolved psychology are partially remedied by the social working out of accepted patterns of conduct.[39]

He goes on to provide excellent extensive and detailed discussion to help clarify our account of moral fog by distinguishing various ways in which moral fog can be generated and obfuscate valuing. He describes two fundamental, general kinds of mistakes: stopping to reflect when one should not stop to do so, and not stopping to reflect when one should. These correspond to a fundamental, general kind of discernment that he says we need for clearing our fog and exercising good judgement: discerning between those cases where it is acceptable to act on habit (or the attitudes we already have and would act on unreflectively) and those cases where we should stop to reflect and revise our habits and standing attitudes (p. 25). He then unpacks what such discernment would involve by describing a decision procedure made by 'appropriately constituted advisory boards' (p. 27). As to how this social method for making better judgements helps the individual, he suggests individuals can simulate how they 'imagine a properly conducted social inquiry would go'. In turn, how well we can do this, he advises, 'will depend on a number of sensitivities', such as our ability to discern options, to tell who will be affected by the options, and to appreciate how they will be affected (p. 27).

We certainly agree that we need to clarify the varieties of moral fog and how they may or may not be cleared. In chapter 4 of *Evil Online*, we describe varieties of moral fog that are generated by different but widely shared features of our nature, such as our learning limitations and vulnerabilities, garden-variety vices and weaknesses, the force of our need to position ourselves well, and for intimate connections. Here we respond to Kitcher's suggestions for further clarity about our account of moral fog by describing how it is sourced in the conditions of subjectivity and contingency of human nature and then further compounded by a variety of 'falsifying veils' generated by other widely shared aspects of self and of relations with others and the world around us.

These sources of fog, we suggest, underpin and explain many of the ways described by Kitcher that we can fail to appreciate value. Thus, for example, the foundational limits and vulnerabilities presented by our subjectivity of focus, along with our contingent possibilities for the exercise of such focus, shape our capacities to appreciate 'when to look and when to leap', to discern the options that are available before us, to discern all of those who will be affected by the options, and to properly appreciate how they will be affected.

---

39. Kitcher, *Losing Your Way in the Fog*, p. 26.

Kitcher also suggests we could go further in characterizing the damage done to quality of life, especially our intimate lives, where our lives are increasingly conducted on screens. In *Evil Online*, we highlight the damage done to quality of life with the collapse of the concurrent, plural worlds of public and private life and the resultant many losses of value and forms of valuing. Again, however, we agree that much more can be said to articulate the nature of the broader impoverishment of our lives as we live 'on screens'. Thus, as we further describe below, one should note some of the large-scale normative losses that arise from the reduction of social spaces online to ones of concealment *or* exposure and some important forms of valuing within intimacy that are lost or perverted online.

Many put our problems online down to unfortunate 'growing pains' from which we will evolve. Others worry we will not get there because they see the danger of becoming hopelessly addicted puppets of algorithms and a milieu created by and designed to serve extraordinarily powerful corporate and political masters.[40] Problems such as addiction, commodification, and manipulation are certainly important current problems, part of the picture of moral regress online. The problems, however, for the future of life online are deeper. Even if we beat addiction and disposed of commodification, manipulation, and a host of other evils online, additional and special problems facing our capacities for value appreciation remain.

The Social Dependence of Valuing

Moral Education and Valuing

Joseph Raz argues there is a very tight dependence of values upon social practice: without relevant social practices (at least somewhere, sometime) the associated values could not exist at all.[41] Christine Korsgaard argues that it is not because of our shared values that we have moral reasons in regard one another, but because of our shared nature, our shared nature as valuers, beings capable of conferring value. Thus, for instance, she says the appreciation of natural beauty need not depend upon social practices supporting such appreciation: 'I think you could be dazzled by a spectacular sunset even if it is the only one you ever

---

40. As mentioned above, this sort of concern is the focus of the film *The Social Dilemma*. For a more nuanced, comprehensive, and beautifully made documentary on the social evils of life online, see *The Cleaners*, dir. Hans Block, Moritz Riesewieck (Gebrueder Beetz Filmproduktion, 2018).

41. Wallace, *The Practice of Value*, pp 15–37.

saw, or if no one in your culture talked about such things'.[42] However, even if we agree with Korsgaard that it is capacities within us rather than forces external to us, like God or culture, that create value, these capacities are limited and vulnerable. We can all agree that for 'quality of consciousness' we invariably need to live in worlds where morally educative social practices help us appreciate value, rather than the contrary.

Iris Murdoch describes how we can be struck by beauty despite our problems. She describes how spotting a kestrel in flight hijacked her consciousness. In Murdoch's case, being struck by beauty took her beyond her preoccupation with self:

> I am looking out my window in an anxious and resentful state of mind, oblivious of my surroundings, brooding perhaps on some damage done to my prestige. Then suddenly I observe a hovering kestrel. In a moment everything is altered. The brooding self with its hurt vanity has disappeared. There is nothing now but kestrel. And when I return to thinking about the other matter it seems less important. And of course this is something which we may also do deliberately: give attention to nature in order to clear our minds of selfish care.[43]

On the other hand, many years ago on a talk show in Australia, a pilot of light planes was describing how he and others would routinely aim and fly their propellers through wedge-tail eagles—for fun. The pilot's story was, of course, a confession. He was highlighting his remarkable lack of appreciation of value, along with that of many comrades in guilt. His world back then was one where the beauty of a wedge-tail eagle in flight was not lost on people. However, it was far less valued, or less clearly so. It was common, for example, for farmers to shoot them to protect their livestock back in the day. Killing them for 'sport' or fun, therefore, would not have been quite the psychological stretch it would be (for most) in more recent times. Falsifying influences, as Murdoch describes, often obscure our perception of value, and in this case they do so for the pilot's being struck by the beauty of the wedge-tail eagle.

Immanuel Kant championed our capacities of reason to appreciate value irrespective of our inclinations (whether cooperative or not) and irrespective of direction from others, social practices, and the world around us. In a well-known description, he describes how such appreciation (the goodwill) would 'shine like

---

42. Wallace, pp. 78–79.
43. Murdoch, p. 88.

a jewel for itself, as something having its full worth in itself'.[44] As well, however, Kant thought that self-conceit (our giving primacy to our 'inclinations' over the moral law) was ubiquitous and significant across human nature.[45] If we are to have any hope in transcending this level of self-conceit, therefore, it seems hard to deny that we can very much do without social practices that celebrate it and the help of robust social practices to help us rise above it.

Moral education has long been a neglected area of philosophical study. This neglect has continued, and now that we find ourselves immersed in the digital age moral education faces significant new problems.[46] These problems arise both because of the fog created by limits and distortions for giving values a presence online and because of the fog created for value appreciation even where users have undertaken significant education regarding the presence of value and disvalue online, such as value for identifying online conduct as bullying or dishonest. It is common, for example, that bullying is undertaken by 'friends' of the victim but that the friends, while quite well-educated about cyberbullying, nevertheless remain relatively clueless in identifying their own conduct as such, often until it is has ended in tragedy and it is all too late.[47]

One of the notable 'falsifying veils' driving our moral fog online are varied aspects of self that drive our long-standing problems with distinguishing what is real from relatively poor imitations, illusions, and substitutes. In *Evil Online*, we describe some of these problems and how we can get lost in such worlds, confusing the virtual and the real. We have always, more or less, created and

---

44. Immanuel Kant, *The Groundwork of the Metaphysic of Morals,* trans. H. J. Paton (New York: HarperCollins, 1964).

45. On our 'radical evil', see Immanuel Kant, 'Religion within the Boundaries of Mere Reason', in *Immanuel Kant: Religion and Rational Authority,* trans. and ed. A. W. Wood and G. Di Giovanni (Cambridge: Cambridge University Press, 1996).

46. In their recent article on new challenges facing moral education in the digital age, Matthew Dennis and Tom Harrison open with a brief, compelling, survey of neglect. They note, for example, that only a single article had previously appeared on the topic of moral education in the 'ever-changing space' of the digital age and that little philosophical reflection has been done on how promoting human flourishing might guide educating for our 'data driven' digital lives. They do suggest also that things seem to be picking up. See Matthew Dennis and Tom Harrison, 'Unique Challenges for the 21st Century: Online Technology and Virtue Education', *Journal of Moral Education,* 2020.

47. For extended discussion of such cases, see Dean Cocking, 'Friendship Online', *Oxford Handbook of Digital Ethics,* ed. Carissa Véliz (Oxford: Oxford University Press, 2021). Education and awareness-raising about other values and disvalues online have also been shown to spectacularly fail to transmit to appreciating those values when online. So, for example, while people have been well-educated on various privacy risks and could demonstrate as much if asked or tested, many nevertheless act as if they are relatively clueless when they get online. See, B. Debatin et al., 'Facebook and Online Privacy: Attitudes, Behaviours and Unintended Consequences', *Journal of Computer-Mediated Communication,* 15, no. 1 (October 2009), pp. 83–108.

lived in 'virtual realities' of a sort, at least worlds well short of the reality or value we claim for them. This can be simply due to our limits of knowledge and understanding or because of the sort of falsifying aspects of self that Murdoch has in mind. So, for example, we pretend a relationship or work-life is good, or good enough, when our anxieties and insecurities are both fueling and being compounded by the illusion. The worry, then, is not just that we might lose sight of realities (moral and otherwise) by living too much in virtual worlds that fail to give these realities sufficient presence. The worry is also that we might want to do so, just as we have often and long wanted to do so in our preonline worlds. Correcting our focus toward reality, exposing the shortcomings of our lives, is often the last thing people want to do. Virtual realities online promise spectacular new ways forward to fuel and compound such desires to deny reality and create 'falsifying veils'.

Our traditional worlds have long been dysfunctional in many notable ways. Approximating personhood has long faced serious, often insurmountable, obstacles. Mortal, much less moral, needs and legitimate claims have been ignored and violated (often on monumental scales). Even in our better sociopolitical worlds, generational poverty, along with drug and alcohol problems and family dysfunction, are common. Laws, courts, and policing are often hijacked and corrupted by power, self-interest, prejudice and shortsightedness, and social and educational services are often unavailable or hard to access for many marginalized groups.

It is important not to lose sight of the dysfunction of our traditional worlds. While online worlds often compound problems of dysfunction (frequently celebrating them as in the case of 'drill music' abovementioned), they can also provide some respite or ways out of traditional world problems. As Dale Dorsey points out, for example, the advent of living online has provided the platform for many victimized and marginalized people and groups to fight back against some of the dysfunction in our traditional worlds. He describes, for instance, some of the great successes of the #MeToo movement (p. 13) and concludes that we must judge the movement to be a very good thing overall. It is, of course, a great good to be able to get some offenders to justice who otherwise would have been able to avoid it and, as Dorsey describes, to have made some significant social changes to long-standing injustices.

Online worlds have provided some important new ways out of the moral fog of our traditional lives and worlds. As we have described here and in *Evil Online*, many aspects of our traditional lives and worlds have long enabled doubling-down on selfing and undermined various values and our appreciation of them. The great successes of the #MeToo movement have redressed some of these failures of our traditional worlds. Notwithstanding such successes, new and fundamental worries about 'doubling-down on selfing' and for value appreciation remain as we increasingly live online. Indeed, even in the case of the #MeToo movement, while it may be good overall, it is not at all clear that the broader culture of online shaming and blaming, freewheeling from the regulatory effects of long-standing laws, norms, and social practices, has been a good thing overall.[48]

Dependence upon Intimates and Society

Aristotle argues that our virtue is socially dependent in two broad ways: upon the help we get from our intimate relations and that from our broader sociopolitical situation. Friendship provides his central illustration of the former. We need friends, he argues, for self-knowledge: 'If, then, it is pleasant to know oneself, and it is not possible to know this without having someone else for a friend, the self-sufficing man will require friendship in order to know himself'.[49]

Second, toward the end of his discussion on moral education, he describes how, even if we have been brought up well to appreciate value, our problems of self, such as our selfishness, will not be extinguished and will need the ongoing support of a broader social system to help reign in these less perfect aspects of ourselves.[50] At this point, he says, our virtue also depends upon the state, and so we need to move to politics and think about what the state must do to meet our needs. If we are to transcend various widely shared weaknesses and vice, then we will need the help of others and our environment, across both our personal and public lives to do so—in particular, through the provision of well-developed morally educative social practices.

Intimate relations, for example (notably friendship), typically enable shared activity that is especially loose and unstructured in a relational context where we are deeply accepted and strongly connected. In so doing, (good) intimate relations provide remedy to some primary wellsprings of our self-conscious anxieties and the falsifying veils they produce. Our strong ties of intimacy provide social spaces for relaxation, experimentation, broad play, and creativity about how to be and act and they deliver some solace from isolation, alienation, and loneliness. In addition, various state actors, functions, and institutions—such as teachers, laws and regulations, and welfare and health services—provide morally educative social practices involving guidance, support, and 'carrots and

---

48. See, for example, Jon Ronson's book on the carnage, *So You've Been Publicly Shamed?* (London: Picador, 2015).

49. Aristotle, *Magna Moralia* (Franklin Classics, 2018), pp. 1213a20–13b.

50. Aristotle, *Nichomachean Ethics*, trans. W. D. Ross, book 10 (Oxford: Oxford University Press, 1980), 1179b39–79b46.

sticks' to help us see through or beyond falsifying veils of self, such as ignorance and self-conceit.

Various writers emphasize the need for social practices and conventions allowing practice, play, experimentation, mistakes, and creativity so that we might develop ourselves and our capacities to engage with others and to contribute generally in worthwhile ways.[51] The pursuit of a worthwhile life involves a lot to experience and figure out, none of which we can do if we cannot do the playing, practicing, trying out, and so on that is required to find and create what we are looking for. We need to ask, for example, Is this right or good? Is another option better? Korsgaard presents Kant's take on the story of Eve and her decision to eat the apple, highlighting that for Kant the story illustrates how we are beings who can define our own ends. We can choose our own way without being 'tied to any single one like other animals'. [52] Thus, irrespective of what our senses tell us, what we are told by others, what is handed down to us by God or culture, is that we can figure things out for ourselves and set our own ends.

Well, we try. However, we must act, engage in choices, and value assessments that give rise to reasons for us, not just, or even so much, as Korsgaard claims, because we are self-conscious beings. Gods do not lack for self-consciousness. Gods, however, do not have to engage in trial and error, try out different interests, relationships, ways of life in the hope of figuring out what matters, discovering and creating value and how we might hold on to it. They need not try to make sense of their situation and come up with a good plan with supporting reasons to deal with it. Gods are self-aware, but they don't have to ask if 'eating the apple' might be permissible, wonder if a better way is possible, and (with some help and luck) come to an appreciation of value. They already know. We, on the other hand, must engage in the 'practicing' and so on, and in getting help from others and our settings, because we are limited in perspective and possibilities for understanding and appreciating value, not simply, or even primarily, because we are self-conscious beings.

Concealment or Exposure Online

In addition to support within our personal lives, such as within friendships, we have also long developed valuable complex and nuanced public social spaces that help support and navigate various expressions of our less-than-autonomous

---

51. See, for example, J. S. Mill's 'experiments in living' in J. S. Mill, *On Liberty*, vol. 18, *The Collected Works of J. S. Mill*, ed. J. M. Robson (Toronto: University of Toronto Press, 1977), pp. 260–67.
52. Korsgaard quotes Kant's take on the story of 'Adam and Eve' as the 'first act of reason', Wallace, *The Practice of Value*, p. 83.

selves. This complexity and nuance of public self-expression and shared activity, however, is largely flatlined on our social media platforms. Our discussion in chapter 3 of *Evil Online* highlights the limits and distortions that the online collapse of the public and private realms presents for the expression of a range of values (such as privacy, autonomy, civility, and intimacy). We cannot expose ourselves in various ways online and expect to have, say, our intimacy or privacy respected by others. In our traditional worlds, however, we have developed social practices over many thousands of years to help us do so, such as by 'putting things aside' or 'social forgetfulness' or 'polite disregard' and other ways to shift the focus of our attention from one another's 'exposure'.

As Thomas Nagel[53] and Ervin Goffman[54] have shown, such public spaces for self-expression are important in many ways. For instance, this kind of nuance and plurality in how we may engage in communication helps us to flag and pick out the attitudes and conduct for which we might be more and less responsible (i.e., the attitudes and conduct that we have more or less voluntarily chosen to present for engagement). Moreover, as we describe in *Evil Online*, our capacities to trust one another often crucially rely upon our having access to the rich, plural, and sometimes conflicting aspects of one another made available by our long inhabiting the nuanced worlds of dynamic face-to-face communication and shared activity in our traditional worlds. Robert Frank, for example, has provided significant evidence of how our perception of commitment and trust in one another depends upon our having such engagement.[55]

These different kinds of public self-expression, and our use of social practices for communication in regard to them, are also crucial for our developing expressions of self and identity. When younger, for instance, we can practice and 'try out' expressions of self in the public realm and make mistakes without too much attention and condemnation. Online, however, we must choose to conceal ourselves altogether or choose to risk exposing ourselves to significant (including negative) public attention and comment.[56]

Carissa Véliz focuses on our discussion in chapter 3 of the moral fog caused by this collapse online of the plural worlds of the public and private realms. In particular, she focuses on our discussion of self-presentation online, how the

53. Thomas Nagel, 'Concealment and Exposure', *Philosophy and Public Affairs*, 27, no. 1 (Winter), 1998.

54. Ervin Goffman, *The Presentation of Self in Everyday Life* (New York, Doubleday Anchor, 1959).

55. See, chapter 3 of *Evil Online* and R. H. Frank, *What Price the Moral High Ground? Ethical Dilemmas in Competitive Environments* (Princeton, NJ: Princeton University Press, 2004).

56. We are imagining here the lack of social practises to 'put things aside' in online public spaces, not talking to a close friend one to one online. In our traditional worlds, of course, people may not 'put things aside' and we may just as well be subject to humiliation and abuse.

illusion of being able to self-present on 'one's own terms' gets special traction online, and how other self-presentations get crowded out or are unavailable. Véliz wants to argue that privacy and control over self-presentation, while closely related, are not the same thing. We agree. After all, one of the main cases we highlight is where respect for privacy can be shown in regard to those presentations of self about which we *do not* have much control. We give an example of being out with a friend, 'bumping' into an 'ex' and their new lover, having some awkward losses of autonomy and exposure of private feelings, and the friend (and the ex) helping out to support our autonomy and respect our privacy. Hence, privacy and control over self-presentation are not the same thing since what is private here concerns feelings over which one does not exercise much control.

Véliz, however, presents the example, and another of ours, to conclude: 'It seems like Cocking and van den Hoven are equating control over self-presentation and privacy. [. . .] As long as we support and do not interfere with people's self-presentation, we are respecting their privacy' (p. 33). As we describe in the example, however, we are interfering with the presentations of awkwardness in order to respect privacy (we suggest by making distracting small talk, wrapping things up quickly and not undertaking more intrusive questioning). Véliz sums up her view of the case this way:

> When, in a social setting, one catches a glimpse of someone's involuntary and revealing gestures that betray some feeling they wish to hide, and one acts with discretion, thereby supporting the person's self-presentation and autonomy, they save their blushes but they are not protecting privacy. Therefore, when a friend encounters her ex and his new lover, and appears so anxious that everyone present notices her negative emotions, to not remark on her nervousness is an act of kindness, but her privacy with respect to her emotions is lost once everyone has noticed her nervousness. Of course, one could make her lose even more privacy by talking to others about this event, but merely refraining from talking about her anxiety to her does not make her regain the privacy she lost with respect to others, her ex, and her ex's lover. (p. 36)

Yes, *some* of her privacy is lost. But it is too swift to leave it at that. It makes an enormous difference how we respond to the exposure—in particular, whether we focus on it and make it our business or we set it aside since it is not any of our business. If we catch someone in a private moment, some of their privacy has thereby been compromised. How we respond can make it much worse or better. We can focus on it and compound the compromising of their privacy, make it a much bigger problem, or we can set it aside as not any of our business and minimize whatever damage is done. As in our example (and Véliz seems to accept), we can respect privacy and minimize the damage by making small talk and wrapping things up quickly in the circumstances.

Véliz suggests that we need to change our culture of overexposure online, of relentless self-presentations. We certainly have a culture of overexposure online, as the 'age of the selfie' attests. On the other hand, we also have a culture of over-concealment as we live online. Our choices are forced, we either expose or conceal, and as a result, much of our rich and broad suite of values and valuing is lost or distorted. Véliz suggests we need a great deal more concealment to better protect privacy and to take away people's control over their self-presentations by changing related conventions and social practices in two ways: by 'having different platforms for different purposes (separating the pursuit of truth, such as in academic platforms, from other kinds of pursuits' (p. 42) and by the presentation of fictitious characters online (and known by users to be fictitious). Since people's roles have been cast for them in these ways, she points out, people will both be better protected against privacy violations and no longer have such control over how they self-present online.

We may well be better off online with far more concealment, given that the choice otherwise risks massive overexposure. Nevertheless, it remains true that to the extent that we live in such worlds, we are far worse off in regards the wide range of our values we have now lost or have distorted on account of our not being able to 'expose ourselves in public' in various ways. There are, of course, many different platforms for many different purposes, and it would be good to make clearer to one and all those platforms that are concerned with truth and those with fiction. As we have been arguing, however, this really is a notable example of the problem (i.e., the fog for our capacities for appreciating reality and value).

Similarly, it might be good to change our conventions for self-presentation online by adopting fictitious characters about which we all are clear, but our capacities for such clarity are the problem. Many users have, in fact, long been engaged in online platforms where they play fictitious characters and where everyone knows that they are the online worlds of avatars. In an early groundbreaking book, *Second Lives: A Journey through Virtual Worlds*, Tim Guest provides in-depth interviews with many users in these worlds. One of the most striking and generally true phenomena shown is how easily and completely many users identify with their fictitious 'second selves'.[57] The fictional nature of many second selves, and everyone being utterly clear about this fact, does not stop them becoming many users' *first* selves. Notoriously, quite generally, as we discuss in

---

57. Tim Guest, *Second Lives: A Journey Through Virtual Worlds* (New York: Random House, 2008).

Evil Online, and above, we have trouble distinguishing the virtual from the real. The worry, then, is some further doubling down on selfing by compounding our fog about reality and illusion.[58]

Our self-presentation and experience of one another in the form of physical human beings has long provided the territory upon which we have built a very sophisticated moral language—a moral language involving a complex suite of physical verbal and nonverbal behaviors. Virtual mediums give limited and distorted traction to this language. As a result, a significant and distinctive problem has emerged for moral understanding, education, and progress in the digital age. The problem is not *just* that we are trying to educate individuals for the practice of values in social worlds where these values are not yet well established. The deeper problem is that with the change in the territory upon which we have developed moral understanding, much of the shared activity and communication that grounds our appreciation of values is absent or misrepresented in these new worlds. Thus, many values and important dimensions of our valuing cannot be well established online. Moral fog is compounded online, both because moral realities and our valuing of them have limited and distorted presence and because, even if present, we are 'doubling down' on selfing and thereby further undermining our capacities to appreciate value.

Kitcher describes the impoverishment of our relational fabric with the loss of 'standing together with one another' in the face of great difficulty as we live online. A general kind of case, which is often not practical online but which has long provided significant help in counteracting some of the corrosive effect life events can bring for value appreciation offline, falls under the heading of just 'being there' with one another. For example, a close friend suffers the devastating loss of a loved one. Nothing much can be said or done to redress the tragedy. However, though one may not do or say much at all, much comfort and solace from the horrendous loneliness, dislocation, and despair the tragedy brings can be delivered by simply 'being there' for the friend. In Australia, for instance, Aboriginal communities have long practiced what they call 'deep listening'[59] for such occasions when nothing much can be said or done to undo terrible damage. What can be done, however, is to be there with someone by deeply listening (without judgement or comment) and thereby provide the psychic space of their not being alone with their tragedy and perhaps help them give some expression

---

58. More generally, as Reverend Dimmesdale notes in *The Scarlet Letter*, we 'cannot wear two hats too long without becoming confused as to which is the real'. Nathaniel Hawthorne, *The Scarlett Letter, A Romance* (Boston, MA: Ticknor, Reed and Fields, 1850).

59. This practice of deep listening is called Dadirri. See, for example, 'Deep Listening (Dadirri)', Creative Spirits, https://www.creativespirits.info/aboriginalculture/education/deep-listening-dadirri [accessed 8 March 2022].

to their trauma.[60] While the loss cannot be resolved, the sort of 'standing together' Kitcher has in mind can be achieved. In so doing, 'being there' for one another provides some antidote to the devastation of a person's valuing capacities that often results from such losses.

We also create valuable social spaces of just being there with one another in various more mundane, everyday ways, such as watching television together or walking in a park. As noted above, good friendships present a paradigm of relatively open, loose, and tolerant social spaces, enabling, for instance, relaxation, day-dreaming, and creative play. In so doing, they provide some proof against some of our 'anxiety-ridden self-consciousness', such as about being lonely, alienated, and disconnected. Just being there with one another serves the same purposes and, in turn, our being able to think beyond our (relatively small-minded) cares or being able to think about them but without the added anxieties of being alone with them.

Conclusion

Moral education and progress in the digital age faces some fundamental and new challenges. Central practices assisting us out of the fog, that help us 'unself' by supporting the dependence of our capacities to appreciate value upon others and the world around us, are largely missing online. As a result, we argued in *Evil Online*, that many of the terrible things flourishing online do so in a surprising way: people with 'an absence of malice', rampant self-interest, criminality, or mental impairment, otherwise morally competent and inclined, can behave appallingly online because their capacities to see value and disvalue become (even more) fogged up. Normative stakes are now obscured that would otherwise (in comparative traditional world settings, such as for the pursuit of friendship) register loud and clear.

There is much work to be done in articulating the nature of our values and how we can give them presence online.[61] Murdoch and Marx, however, offer important guidance by getting us to notice the different, but very widely shared, ways in which we fail to see value or disvalue, even if it right is in front of us, and by directing us to the culprit: the falsifying veils of self, others, and the

---

60. For some powerful examples, see Judy Atkinson's talk, 'The Value of Deep Listening—Aboriginal Gift to the Nation', TEDxSydney, 16 June 2017, https://tedxsydney.com/talk/the-value-of-deep-listening-the-aboriginal-gift-to-the-nation-judy-atkinson/

61. At the end of *Evil Online*, we make the call for better value-sensitive design of our online spaces. Dorsey gives the example of Reddit, which is one good illustration of better value-sensitive design.

world around us. The future for value-sensitive design of life online, therefore, requires focus well beyond identifying our values and giving them a presence in online settings. Indeed, the design focus needs to be primarily on our capacities to appreciate value and identifying practices to enable them. To undertake this, we have argued, we need to better understand our problems with value appreciation, and we have argued that the problem of moral fog presents one of these foundational problems.

In addition to the need to focus more on designing online settings to provide social practices to better enable the *appreciation* of realities and values, we have also suggested that many values, or important aspects of them, cannot transfer online. Thus, in addition to creating ways in which values can have presence, and ways in which our valuing of them can be enabled in the very different terrain of online communication, value-sensitive design of our lives in an increasingly online world should also focus on identifying values the appreciation of which cannot, or cannot well, be replicated online and how the pursuit of these values may be better supported offline—the online social revolution kicked off by hijacking and derailing friendship. Reclaiming friendship, then, would be a good place to start.

Printed in the USA
CPSIA information can be obtained
at www.ICGtesting.com
LVHW081548040924
790119LV00014B/552